P9-CQC-954

The Consequences of Modernity

The Raymond Fred West Memorial Lectures
at Stanford University

The Raymond Fred West Memorial Lectures
on Immortality, Human Conduct, and Human Destiny
were established in 1910 by Mr. and Mrs. Fred West of Seattle
in memory of their son

The Consequences
of Modernity

Anthony Giddens

Stanford University Press
Stanford, California

Stanford University Press, Stanford, California
© 1990 by the Board of Trustees of the
Leland Stanford Junior University
Printed in the United States of America
Original printing 1990
Last figure below indicates year of this printing:
00   99   98   97   96   95   94   93   92   91

Library of Congress Cataloging-in-Publication Data

Giddens, Anthony.
   The consequences of modernity/ Anthony Giddens.
p.   cm.
ISBN 0-8047-1762-I (alk. paper)
ISBN 0-8047-1891-1 (pbk: alk. paper)
      I. Social structure.   2. Civilization, Modern.
3. Postmodernism.   I. Title.
HM131.G397   1990   89-62426
303.44 -dc20   CIP

∞   This book is printed on acid-free paper.

Preface

This book essentially takes the form of an extended essay. I have divided it up into sections, rather than formal chapters, in order to develop the flow of the arguments in an uninterrupted fashion. The ideas expressed herein are directly bound up with my previous writings, and I have often made reference to these. I hope the reader will understand and forgive such frequent self-referencing, which is intended not as hubris but as a mode of providing backing for claims that cannot be exhaustively defended in a work of this brevity. The book began life in the shape of the Raymond Fred West Memorial Lectures, which I delivered at Stanford University, California, in April 1988. I am very grateful to my hosts at Stanford on that occasion, whose welcome and hospitality was wonderful. In particular, I am indebted to Grant Barnes, of Stanford University Press, who was instrumental in gaining me the invitation to give the lectures and without whom this work would not exist.

Contents

I

1

II

55

III

79

IV
112

V
151

VI
174

Figures and Tables

Figures

Tables

What if this present were the world's last night?

John Donne, *Devotions upon Emergent Occasions*

———

Imaginary time is indistinguishable from directions in space. If one can go north, one can turn around and head south; equally, if one can go forward in imaginary time, one ought to be able to turn around and go backward. This means that there can be no important difference between the forward and backward directions of imaginary time. On the other hand, when one looks at "real" time, there's a very big difference between the forward and backward directions, as we all know. Where does this difference between the past and the future come from? Why do we remember the past but not the future?

Stephen W. Hawking, *A Brief History of Time*

———

In March 1986, a nine-page article about the Chernobyl nuclear installation appeared in the English-language edition of *Soviet Life*, under the heading of 'Total Safety'. Only a month later, over the weekend of the 26–27 April, the world's worst nuclear accident—thus far—occurred at the plant.

James Bellini, *High Tech Holocaust*

———

When we discover that there are several cultures instead of just one and consequently at the time when we acknowledge the end of a sort of cultural monopoly, be it illusory or real, we are threatened with the destruction of our own discovery. Suddenly it becomes possible that there are just *others*, that we ourselves are an 'other' among others. All meaning and every goal having disappeared, it becomes possible to wander through civilisations as if through vestiges and ruins. The whole of mankind becomes an imaginary museum: where shall we go this weekend—visit the Angkor ruins or take a stroll in Tivoli of Copenhagen? Paul Ricoeur, "Civilisations and National Cultures," in his *History and Truth*

The Consequences of Modernity

I

Introduction

In what follows I shall develop an institutional analysis
of modernity with cultural and epistemological over-
tones. In so doing, I differ substantially from most current
discussions, in which these emphases are reversed. What
is modernity? As a first approximation, let us simply say
the following: "modernity" refers to modes of social life
or organisation which emerged in Europe from about the
seventeenth century onwards and which subsequently became more or less worldwide in their influence. This associates modernity with a time period and with an initial
geographical location, but for the moment leaves its major characteristics safely stowed away in a black box.

Today, in the late twentieth century, it is argued by
many, we stand at the opening of a new era, to which the
social sciences must respond and which is taking us beyond modernity itself. A dazzling variety of terms has
been suggested to refer to this transition, a few of which
refer positively to the emergence of a new type of social
system (such as the "information society" or the "consumer society") but most of which suggest rather that a

preceding state of affairs is drawing to a close ("post-modernity," "post-modernism," "post-industrial society," "post-capitalism," and so forth). Some of the debates about these matters concentrate mainly upon institutional transformations, particularly those which propose that we are moving from a system based upon the manufacture of material goods to one concerned more centrally with information. More commonly, however, these controversies are focused largely upon issues of philosophy and epistemology. This is the characteristic outlook, for example, of the author who has been primarily responsible for popularising the notion of post-modernity, Jean-François Lyotard.[1] As he represents it, post-modernity refers to a shift away from attempts to ground epistemology and from faith in humanly engineered progress. The condition of post-modernity is distinguished by an evaporating of the "grand narrative"— the overarching "story line" by means of which we are placed in history as beings having a definite past and a predictable future. The post-modern outlook sees a plurality of heterogeneous claims to knowledge, in which science does not have a privileged place.

A standard response to the sort of ideas expressed by Lyotard is to seek to demonstrate that a coherent epistemology is possible—and that generalisable knowledge about social life and patterns of social development can be achieved.[2] But I want to take a different tack. The disorientation which expresses itself in the feeling that systematic knowledge about social organisation cannot be obtained, I shall argue, results primarily from the sense many of us have of being caught up in a universe of events we do not fully understand, and which seems in large part outside of our control. To analyse how this has come to be the case, it is not sufficient merely to invent new terms, like post-modernity and the rest. Instead, we have to look again at the nature of modernity itself which, for certain fairly specific reasons, has been poorly grasped in the social sciences hitherto. Rather than entering a period of post-modernity, we are moving into one in which the consequences of modernity are becoming more radicalised and universalised than before. Beyond modernity, I shall claim, we can perceive the contours of a new and different order, which is "post-modern"; but this is quite distinct from what is at the moment called by many "post-modernity."

The views I shall develop have their point of origin in what I have elsewhere called a "discontinuist" interpretation of modern social development.[3] By this I mean that modern social institutions are in some respects unique—distinct in form from all types of traditional order. Capturing the nature of the discontinuities involved, I shall argue, is a necessary preliminary to analysing what modernity actually is, as well as diagnosing its consequences for us in the present day.

My approach also demands a brief critical discussion of some of the dominant standpoints in sociology, as the discipline most integrally involved with the study of modern social life. Given their cultural and epistemological orientation, the debates about modernity and post-modernity for the most part have not confronted the shortcomings in established sociological positions. An interpretation concerned mainly with institutional analysis, however, as my discussion is, must do so.

Using these observations as a springboard, in the bulk

of this study I shall attempt to provide a fresh characterisation both of the nature of modernity and of the post-
modern order which might emerge on the other side of
the current era.

The Discontinuities of Modernity

The idea that human history is marked by certain "discontinuities" and does not have a smoothly developing
form is of course a familiar one and has been stressed in
most versions of Marxism. My use of the term has no particular connection with historical materialism, however,
and is not directed at characterising human history as a
whole. There undoubtedly are discontinuities at various
phases of historical development—as, for example, at the
points of transition between tribal societies and the emergence of agrarian states. I am not concerned with these. I
wish instead to accentuate that particular discontinuity,
or set of discontinuities, associated with the modern period.

The modes of life brought into being by modernity
have swept us away from *all* traditional types of social
order, in quite unprecedented fashion. In both their ex-
tensionality and their intensionality the transformations
involved in modernity are more profound than most sorts
of change characteristic of prior periods. On the extensional plane they have served to establish forms of social
interconnection which span the globe; in intensional
terms they have come to alter some of the most intimate
and personal features of our day-to-day existence. Obviously there are continuities between the traditional and
the modern, and neither is cut of whole cloth; it is well
known how misleading it can be to contrast these two in

4

too gross a fashion. But the changes occurring over the past three or four centuries—a tiny period of historical time—have been so dramatic and so comprehensive in their impact that we get only limited assistance from our knowledge of prior periods of transition in trying to interpret them.

The long-standing influence of social evolutionism is one of the reasons why the discontinuist character of modernity has often not been fully appreciated. Even those theories which stress the importance of discontinuist transitions, like that of Marx, see human history as having an overall direction, governed by general dynamic principles. Evolutionary theories do indeed represent "grand narratives," although not necessarily ones which are teleologically inspired. According to evolutionism, "history" can be told in terms of a "story line" which imposes an orderly picture upon the jumble of human happenings. History "begins" with small, isolated cultures of hunters and gatherers, moves through the development of crop-growing and pastoral communities and from there to the formation of agrarian states, culminating in the emergence of modern societies in the West.

Displacing the evolutionary narrative, or deconstructing its story line, not only helps to clarify the task of analysing modernity, it also refocuses part of the debate about the so-called post-modern. History does not have the "totalised" form attributed to it by evolutionary conceptions—and evolutionism, in one version or another, has been far more influential in social thought than the teleological philosophies of history which Lyotard and others take as their prime objects of attack. Deconstructing social evolutionism means accepting that history cannot be seen as a unity, or as reflecting certain unifying principles of organisation and transformation. But it does not imply that all is chaos or that an infinite number of purely idiosyncratic "histories" can be written. There are definite episodes of historical transition, for example, whose character can be identified and about which generalisations can be made.[4]

How should we identify the discontinuities which separate modern social institutions from the traditional social orders? Several features are involved. One is the sheer *pace of change* which the era of modernity sets into motion. Traditional civilisations may have been considerably more dynamic than other pre-modern systems, but the rapidity of change in conditions of modernity is extreme. If this is perhaps most obvious in respect of technology, it also pervades all other spheres. A second discontinuity is the *scope of change*. As different areas of the globe are drawn into interconnection with one another, waves of social transformation crash across virtually the whole of the earth's surface. A third feature concerns the intrinsic *nature of modern institutions*. Some modern social forms are simply not found in prior historical periods—such as the political system of the nation-state, the wholesale dependence of production upon inanimate power sources, or the thoroughgoing commodification of products and wage labour. Others only have a specious continuity with pre-existing social orders. An example is the city. Modern urban settlements often incorporate the sites of traditional cities, and it may look as though they have merely spread out from them. In fact, modern urbanism is ordered according to quite different principles from those which set off the pre-modern city from the countryside in prior periods.[5]

Security and Danger, Trust and Risk

In pursuing my enquiry into the character of modernity, I want to concentrate a substantial portion of the discussion upon the themes of *security versus danger* and *trust versus risk*. Modernity, as everyone living in the closing years of the twentieth century can see, is a double-edged phenomenon. The development of modern social institutions and their worldwide spread have created vastly greater opportunities for human beings to enjoy a secure and rewarding existence than any type of pre-modern system. But modernity also has a sombre side, which has become very apparent in the present century.

On the whole, the "opportunity side" of modernity was stressed most strongly by the classical founders of sociology. Marx and Durkheim both saw the modern era as a troubled one. But each believed that the beneficent possibilities opened up by the modern era outweighed its negative characteristics. Marx saw class struggle as the source of fundamental schisms in the capitalistic order, but at the same time envisaged the emergence of a more humane social system. Durkheim believed the further expansion of industrialism would establish a harmonious and fulfilling social life, integrated through a combination of the division of labour and moral individualism. Max Weber was the most pessimistic among the three founding fathers, seeing the modern world as a paradoxical one in which material progress was obtained only at the cost of an expansion of bureaucracy that crushed individual creativity and autonomy. Yet even he did not fully anticipate how extensive the darker side of modernity would turn out to be.

To take an example, all three authors saw that modern industrial work had degrading consequences, subjecting many human beings to the discipline of dull, repetitive labour. But it was not foreseen that the furthering of the "forces of production" would have large-scale destructive potential in relation to the material environment. Ecological concerns do not brook large in the traditions of thought incorporated into sociology, and it is not surprising that sociologists today find it hard to develop a systematic appraisal of them.

A second example is the consolidated use of political power, particularly as demonstrated in episodes of totalitarianism. The arbitrary use of political power seemed to the sociological founders to belong primarily to the past (although sometimes having echoes in the present, as indicated in Marx's analysis of the rule of Louis Napoleon). "Despotism" appeared to be mainly characteristic of premodern states. In the wake of the rise of fascism, the Holocaust, Stalinism, and other episodes of twentieth-century history, we can see that totalitarian possibilities are contained within the institutional parameters of modernity rather than being foreclosed by them. Totalitarianism is distinct from traditional despotism, but is all the more frightening as a result. Totalitarian rule connects political, military, and ideological power in more concentrated form than was ever possible before the emergence of modern nation-states.[6]

The development of military power as a general phenomenon provides a further case in point. Durkheim and Weber both lived to witness the horrendous events of the First World War, although Durkheim died before the war reached its conclusion. The conflict shattered the anticipation Durkheim had previously held that a pacific, integrated industrial order would naturally be promoted by industrialism and proved impossible to accommodate within the intellectual framework he had developed as the basis of his sociology. Weber gave more attention to the role of military power in past history than did either Marx or Durkheim. Yet he did not elaborate an account of the military in modern times, shifting the burden of his analysis towards rationalisation and bureaucratisation. None of the classical founders of sociology gave systematic attention to the phenomenon of the "industrialisation of war."[7]

Social thinkers writing in the late nineteenth and early twentieth centuries could not have foreseen the invention of nuclear weaponry.* But the connecting of industrial innovation and organisation to military power is a process that dates back to the early origins of modern industrialisation itself. That this went largely unanalysed in sociology is an indication of the strength of the view that the newly emergent order of modernity would be essentially pacific, in contrast to the militarism that had characterised previous ages. Not just the threat of nuclear confrontation, but the actuality of military conflict, form a basic part of the "dark side" of modernity in the current century. The twentieth century is the century of war, with

*Yet, writing in 1914, just before the outbreak of the Great War, H. G. Wells did make such a prediction, influenced by the physicist Frederick Soddy, a collaborator of Ernest Rutherford. Wells's book, *The World Set Free*, recounts the story of a war which erupts in Europe in 1958, from there spreading throughout the world. In the war, a terrible weapon is used, constructed from a radioactive substance called Carolinum. Hundreds of these bombs, which Wells called "atomic bombs," are dropped on the world's cities, causing immense devastation. A time of mass starvation and political chaos follows, after which a new world republic is set up, in which war is forever prohibited.

the number of serious military engagements involving substantial loss of life being considerably higher than in either of the two preceding centuries. In the present century thus far, over 100 million people have been killed in wars, a higher proportion of the world's population than in the nineteenth century, even allowing for overall population increase.[8] Should even a limited nuclear engagement be fought, the loss of life would be staggering, and a full superpower conflict might eradicate humanity altogether.

The world in which we live today is a fraught and dangerous one. This has served to do more than simply blunt or force us to qualify the assumption that the emergence of modernity would lead to the formation of a happier and more secure social order. Loss of a belief in "progress," of course, is one of the factors that underlies the dissolution of "narratives" of history. Yet there is much more at stake here than the conclusion that history "goes nowhere." We have to develop an institutional analysis of the double-edged character of modernity. In so doing, we must make good some of the limitations of the classical sociological perspectives, limitations which have continued to affect sociological thought in the present day.

Sociology and Modernity

Sociology is a very broad and diverse subject, and any simple generalisations about it as a whole are questionable. But we can point to three widely held conceptions, deriving in some part from the continuing impact of classical social theory in sociology, which inhibit a satisfactory analysis of modern institutions. The first concerns the institutional diagnosis of modernity; the second has to do with the prime focus of sociological analysis, "society"; the third relates to the connections between sociological knowledge and the characteristics of modernity to which such knowledge refers.

1. The most prominent theoretical traditions in sociology, including those stemming from the writings of Marx, Durkheim, and Weber, have tended to look to a single overriding dynamic of transformation in interpreting the nature of modernity. For authors influenced by Marx, the major transformative force shaping the modern world is capitalism. With the decline of feudalism, agrarian production based in the local manor is replaced by production for markets of national and international scope, in terms of which not only an indefinite variety of material goods but also human labour power become commodified. The emergent social order of modernity is *capitalistic* in both its economic system and its other institutions. The restless, mobile character of modernity is explained as an outcome of the investment-profit-investment cycle which, combined with the overall tendency of the rate of profit to decline, brings about a constant disposition for the system to expand.

This viewpoint was criticised both by Durkheim and by Weber, who helped initiate rival interpretations that have strongly influenced subsequent sociological analysis. In the tradition of Saint-Simon, Durkheim traced the nature of modern institutions primarily to the impact of *industrialism*. For Durkheim, capitalistic competition is not the central element of the emerging industrial order, and some of the characteristics upon which Marx laid great stress he saw as marginal and transitory. The rapidly changing character of modern social life does not derive essentially from capitalism, but from the energising impulse of a complex division of labour, harnessing production to human needs through the industrial exploitation of nature. We live, not in a capitalist, but in an industrial order.

Weber spoke of "capitalism," rather than the existence of an industrial order, but in some key respects his view is closer to Durkheim than to Marx. "Rational capitalism" as Weber characterizes it, comprises the economic mechanisms specified by Marx, including the commodification of wage labour. Yet "capitalism" in this usage plainly means something different from the same term as it appears in Marx's writings. "Rationalisation," as expressed in technology and in the organisation of human activities, in the shape of bureaucracy, is the keynote.

Do we now live in a capitalist order? Is industrialism the dominant force shaping the institutions of modernity? Should we rather look to the rationalised control of information as the chief underlying characteristic? I shall argue that these questions cannot be answered in this form—that is to say, we should not regard these as mutually exclusive characterisations. Modernity, I propose, is *multidimensional on the level of institutions*, and each of the elements specified by these various traditions plays some part.

2. The concept of "society" occupies a focal position in much sociological discourse. "Society" is of course an ambiguous notion, referring both to "social association" in a generic way and to a distinct system of social relations. I am concerned here only with the second of these usages, which certainly figures in a basic fashion in each of the dominant sociological perspectives. While Marxist authors may sometimes favour the term "social forma-

tion" over that of "society," the connotation of "bounded system" is similar.

In non-Marxist perspectives, particularly those connected with the influence of Durkheim, the concept of society is bound up with the very definition of sociology itself. The conventional definition of sociology with which virtually every textbook opens—"sociology is the study of human societies" or "sociology is the study of modern societies"—gives clear expression to this view. Few, if any, contemporary writers follow Durkheim in treating society in an almost mystical way, as a sort of "superbeing" to which individual members quite properly display an attitude of awe. But the primacy of "society" as the core notion of sociology is very broadly accepted.

Why should we have reservations about the notion of society as ordinarily utilised in sociological thought? There are two reasons. Even where they do not explicitly say so, authors who regard sociology as the study of "societies" have in mind the societies associated with modernity. In conceptualising them, they think of quite clearly delimited systems, which have their own inner unity. Now, understood in this way, "societies" are plainly *nation-states*. Yet although a sociologist speaking of a particular society might casually employ instead the term "nation," or "country," the character of the nation-state is rarely directly theorised. In explicating the nature of modern societies, we have to capture the specific characteristics of the nation-state—a type of social community which contrasts in a radical way with pre-modern states.

A second reason concerns certain theoretical interpretations that have been closely connected with the notion of society. One of the most influential of these is that given by Talcott Parsons.⁹ According to Parsons, the preeminent objective of sociology is to resolve the "problem of order." The problem of order is central to the interpretation of the boundedness of social systems, because it is defined as a question of integration—what holds the system together in the face of divisions of interest which would "set all against all."

I do not think it is useful to think of social systems in such a way.¹⁰ We should reformulate the question of order as a problem of how it comes about that social systems "bind" time and space. The problem of order is here seen as one of *time-space distanciation*—the conditions under which time and space are organised so as to connect presence and absence. This issue has to be conceptually distinguished from that of the "boundedness" of social systems. Modern societies (nation-states), in some respects at any rate, have a clearly defined boundedness. But all such societies are also interwoven with ties and connections which crosscut the sociopolitical system of the state and the cultural order of the "nation." Virtually no premodern societies were as clearly bounded as modern nation-states. Agrarian civilisations had "frontiers," in the sense attributed to that term by geographers, while smaller agricultural communities and hunting and gathering societies normally shaded off into other groups around them and were not territorial in the same sense as state-based societies.

In conditions of modernity, the level of time-space distanciation is much greater than in even the most developed of agrarian civilisations. But there is more than a simple expansion in the capability of social systems to span time and space. We must look in some depth at how modern institutions become "situated" in time and space to identify some of the distinctive traits of modernity as a whole.

3. In various otherwise divergent forms of thought, sociology has been understood as generating knowledge about modern social life which can be used in the interests of prediction and control. Two versions of this theme are prominent. One is the view that sociology supplies information about social life which can give us a kind of control over social institutions similar to that which the physical sciences provide in the realm of nature. Sociological knowledge is believed to stand in an instrumental relation to the social world to which it relates; such knowledge can be applied in a technological fashion to intervene in social life. Other authors, including Marx (or, at least, Marx according to certain interpretations) have taken a different standpoint. For them, the idea of "using history to make history" is the key: the findings of social science cannot just be applied to an inert subject matter, but have to be filtered through the self-understandings of social agents.

This latter view is undeniably more sophisticated than the other, but it is still inadequate, since its conception of reflexivity is too simple. The relation between sociology and its subject matter—the actions of human beings in conditions of modernity—has to be understood instead in terms of the "double hermeneutic."[11] The development of sociological knowledge is parasitical upon lay agents' concepts; on the other hand, notions coined in the meta-languages of the social sciences routinely reenter the universe of actions they were initially formulated to describe or account for. But it does not lead in a direct way to a transparent social world. *Sociological knowledge spirals in and out of the universe of social life, reconstructing both itself and that universe as an integral part of that process.*

This is a model of reflexivity, but not one in which there is a parallel track between the accumulation of sociological knowledge on the one side and the steadily more extensive control of social development on the other. Sociology (and the other social sciences which deal with extant human beings) does not develop cumulative knowledge in the same way as the natural sciences might be said to do. Per contra, the "feed-in" of sociological notions or knowledge claims into the social world is not a process that can be readily channeled, either by those who propose them or even by powerful groups or governmental agencies. Yet the practical impact of social science and sociological theories is enormous, and sociological concepts and findings are constitutively involved in what modernity *is*. I shall develop the significance of this point in some detail below.

If we are adequately to grasp the nature of modernity, I want to argue, we have to break away from existing sociological perspectives in each of the respects mentioned. We have to account for the extreme dynamism and globalising scope of modern institutions and explain the nature of their discontinuities from traditional cultures. I shall come to a characterisation of these institutions later, first of all posing the question: what are the sources of the dynamic nature of modernity? Several sets of elements can be distinguished in formulating an answer, each of which is relevant both to the dynamic and to the "world-embracing" character of modern institutions.

The dynamism of modernity derives from the *separation of time and space* and their recombination in forms which permit the precise time-space "zoning" of social life; the *disembedding* of social systems (a phenomenon which connects closely with the factors involved in time-space separation); and the *reflexive ordering and reordering* of social relations in the light of continual inputs of knowledge affecting the actions of individuals and groups. I shall analyse these in some detail (which will include an initial look at the nature of trust), beginning with the ordering of time and space.

Modernity, Time, and Space

To understand the intimate connections between modernity and the transformation of time and space, we have to start by drawing some contrasts with time-space relations in the pre-modern world.

All pre-modern cultures possessed modes of the calculation of time. The calendar, for example, was as distinctive a feature of agrarian states as the invention of writing. But the time reckoning which formed the basis of day-to-day life, certainly for the majority of the population, always linked time with place—and was usually imprecise and variable. No one could tell the time of day without reference to other socio-spatial markers: "when" was almost universally either connected with "where" or identified by regular natural occurrences. The invention of the mechanical clock and its diffusion to virtually all members of the population (a phenomenon which dates at its earliest from the late eighteenth century) were of key significance in the separation of time from space. The clock expressed a uniform dimension of "empty" time, quantified in such a way as to permit the precise designation of "zones" of the day (e.g., the "working day").[12]

Time was still connected with space (and place) until

17

the uniformity of time measurement by the mechanical clock was matched by uniformity in the social organisation of time. This shift coincided with the expansion of modernity and was not completed until the current century. One of its main aspects is the worldwide standardisation of calendars. Everyone now follows the same dating system: the approach of the "year 2000," for example, is a global event. Different "New Years" continue to co-exist but are subsumed within a mode of dating which has become to all intents and purposes universal. A second aspect is the standardising of time across regions. Even in the latter part of the nineteenth century, different areas within a single state usually had different "times," while between the borders of states the situation was even more chaotic.[13]

The "emptying of time" is in large part the precondition for the "emptying of space" and thus has causal priority over it. For, as I shall argue below, coordination across time is the basis of the control of space. The development of "empty space" may be understood in terms of the separation of *space* from *place*. It is important to stress the distinction between these two notions, because they are often used as more or less synonymous with one another. "Place" is best conceptualised by means of the idea of locale, which refers to the physical settings of social activity as situated geographically.[14] In pre-modern societies, space and place largely coincide, since the spatial dimensions of social life are, for most of the population, and in most respects, dominated by "presence"—by localised activities. The advent of modernity increasingly tears space away from place by fostering relations between "absent" others, locationally distant from any given situation of face-to-face interaction. In conditions of modernity, place becomes increasingly *phantasmago-ric*: that is to say, locales are thoroughly penetrated by and shaped in terms of social influences quite distant from them. What structures the locale is not simply that which is present on the scene; the "visible form" of the locale conceals the distanciated relations which determine its nature.

The dislocation of space from place is not, as in the case of time, closely bound up with the emergence of uniform modes of measurement. Means of reliably subdividing space have always been more readily available than means of producing uniform measures of time. The development of "empty space" is linked above all to two sets of factors: those allowing for the representation of space without reference to a privileged locale which forms a distinct vantage-point; and those making possible the substitutability of different spatial units. The "discovery" of "remote" regions of the world by Western travelers and explorers was the necessary basis of both of these. The progressive charting of the globe that led to the creation of universal maps, in which perspective played little part in the representation of geographical position and form, established space as "independent" of any particular place or region.

The separation of time from space should not be seen as a unilinear development, in which there are no reversals or which is all-encompassing. On the contrary, like all trends of development, it has dialectical features, provoking opposing characteristics. Moreover, the severing of time from space provides a basis for their recombination in relation to social activity. This is easily demonstrated by taking the example of the timetable. A timetable, such as a schedule of the times at which trains run, might seem at first sight to be merely a temporal chart. But actually it is a time-space ordering device, indicating both when and where trains arrive. As such, it permits the complex coordination of trains and their passengers and freight across large tracts of time-space.

Why is the separation of time and space so crucial to the extreme dynamism of modernity?

First, it is the prime condition of the processes of disembedding which I shall shortly analyse. The separating of time and space and their formation into standardised, "empty" dimensions cut through the connections between social activity and its "embedding" in the particularities of contexts of presence. Disembedded institutions greatly extend the scope of time-space distanciation and, to have this effect, depend upon coordination across time and space. This phenomenon serves to open up manifold possibilities of change by breaking free from the restraints of local habits and practices.

Second, it provides the gearing mechanisms for that distinctive feature of modern social life, the rationalised organisation. Organisations (including modern states) may sometimes have the rather static, inertial quality which Weber associated with bureaucracy, but more commonly they have a dynamism that contrasts sharply with pre-modern orders. Modern organisations are able to connect the local and the global in ways which would have been unthinkable in more traditional societies and in so doing routinely affect the lives of many millions of people.

Third, the radical historicity associated with modernity depends upon modes of "insertion" into time and space unavailable to previous civilisations. "History," as the systematic appropriation of the past to help shape the future, received its first major stimulus with the early emergence of agrarian states, but the development of modern institutions gave it a fundamentally new impetus. A standardised dating system, now universally acknowledged, provides for an appropriation of a unitary past, however much such "history" may be subject to contrasting interpretations. In addition, given the overall mapping of the globe that is today taken for granted, the unitary past is one which is worldwide; time and space are recombined to form a genuinely world-historical framework of action and experience.

Disembedding

Let me now move on to consider the disembedding of social systems. By disembedding I mean the "lifting out" of social relations from local contexts of interaction and their restructuring across indefinite spans of time-space.

Sociologists have often discussed the transition from the traditional to the modern world in terms of the concepts of "differentiation" or "functional specialisation." The movement from small-scale systems to agrarian civilisations and then to modern societies, according to this view, can be seen as a process of progressive inner diversification. Various objections can be made to this position. It tends to be linked to an evolutionary outlook, gives no attention to the "boundary problem" in the analysis of societal systems, and quite often depends upon functionalist notions.[15] More important to the present discussion, however, is the fact that it does not satisfactorily address the issue of time-space distanciation. The notions of differentiation or functional specialisation are not well suited to handling the phenomenon of the bracketing of time and space by social systems. The image evoked by disembedding is better able to capture the shifting alignments of time and space which are of elementary importance for social change in general and for the nature of modernity in particular.

I want to distinguish two types of disembedding mechanisms intrinsically involved in the development of modern social institutions. The first of these I refer to as the creation of *symbolic tokens*; the second I shall call the establishment of *expert systems*.

By symbolic tokens I mean media of interchange which can be "passed around" without regard to the specific characteristics of individuals or groups that handle them at any particular juncture. Various kinds of symbolic tokens can be distinguished, such as media of political legitimacy; I shall concentrate here upon the token of *money*.

The nature of money has been widely discussed in sociology and obviously forms an abiding concern of economics. In his early writings, Marx spoke of money as "the universal whore," a medium of exchange which negates the content of goods or services by substituting for them an impersonal standard. Money permits the exchange of anything for anything, regardless of whether the goods involved share any substantive qualities in common with one another. Marx's critical comments on money foreshadow his subsequent distinction between use-value and exchange-value. Money makes possible the generalisation of the second of these because of its role as a "pure commodity."[16]

The most far-reaching and sophisticated account of the connections between money and modernity, however, is that written by Georg Simmel.[17] I shall return to this shortly, since I shall draw upon it in my own discussion of money as a disembedding mechanism. In the meantime, it should be noted that a concern with the social character of money forms part of the writings of Talcott Parsons and Niklas Luhmann in more recent times. Parsons is the dominant author here. According to him, money is one of several types of "circulating media" in modern societies, others of which include power and language. Although the approaches of Parsons and Luhmann have some affinities with that which I shall set out below, I do not accept the main framework of their analyses. Neither power nor language is on a par with money or other disembedding mechanisms. Power and the use of language are intrinsic features of social action on a very general level, not specific social forms.

What is money? Economists have never been able to agree about an answer to this question. Keynes's writings, however, probably supply the best starting point. One of Keynes's main emphases is upon the distinctive character of money, the rigorous analysis of which separates his work from those versions of neo-classical economic thought in which, as Leon Walras puts it, "money does not exist."[18] Keynes first of all distinguishes between money of account and money proper.[19] In its early form, money is identified with debt. "Commodity money" thus designated is a first step along the way in the transformation of barter into a money economy. A basic transition is initiated when acknowledgments of debt can be substituted for commodities as such in the settlement of transactions. This "spontaneous acknowledgment of debt" can be issued by any bank and represents "bank money." Bank money is recognition of a private debt until it becomes more widely diffused. This movement to money proper involves the intervention of the state, which acts as the guarantor of value. Only the state (which means here the modern nation-state) is able to transform private debt transactions into a standard means of payment—in other words, to bring debt and credit into balance in respect of an indefinite number of transactions.

Money in its developed form is thus defined above all in terms of credit and debt, where these concern a plurality of widely scattered interchanges. It is for this reason that Keynes relates money closely to time.[20] Money is a mode of deferral, providing the means of connecting credit and liability in circumstances where immediate exchange of products is impossible. Money, we can say, is a means of bracketing time and so of lifting transactions out of particular milieux of exchange. More accurately put, in the terms introduced earlier, money is a means of time-space distanciation. Money provides for the enactment of transactions between agents widely separated in time and space. The spatial implications of money are well characterised by Simmel, who points out:

the role of money is associated with the spatial distance between the individual and his possession. . . . Only if the profit of an enterprise takes a form that can be easily transferred to any other place does it guarantee to property and the owner, through their spatial separation, a high degree of independence or, in other words, self-mobility. . . . The power of money to bridge distances enables the owner and his possessions to exist so far apart that each of them may follow their own precepts to a greater extent than in the period when the owner and his possessions still stood in a direct mutual relationship, when every economic engagement was also a personal one.[21]

The disembeddedness provided for in modern money economies is vastly greater than was the case in any of the pre-modern civilisations in which money existed. Even in the most developed of monetary systems in the pre-modern era, such as that of the Roman Empire, no advance was made beyond what in Keynes's terms would be commodity money, in the shape of material coinage. Today, "money proper" is independent of the means whereby it is represented, taking the form of pure information lodged as figures in a computer printout. It is the wrong metaphor to see money, as Parsons does, as a circulating medium. As coinage or cash, money circulates; but in a modern economic order the large bulk of monetary transactions do not take this form. Cencini points out that the conventional ideas that money "circulates," and can be thought of as a "flow," are essentially misleading.[22] If money flowed—say, like water—its circulation would be expressed directly in terms of time. It would follow from this that the greater the velocity, the narrower the stream needed for the same quantity to flow per unit of time. In the case of money, this would mean that the amount required for a given transaction would be proportional to the velocity of its circulation. But it is plainly nonsense to say that payment of £100 could equally well be carried out with £50 or £10. Money does not relate to time (or, more accurately, time-space) as a flow, but precisely as a means of bracketing time-space by coupling instantaneity and deferral, presence and absence. In R. S. Sayers's words, "No asset is in action as a medium of exchange except in the very moment of being transferred from one ownership to another, in settlement of some transaction."[23]

Money is an example of the disembedding mechanisms associated with modernity; I shall not attempt to detail the substantive contribution of a developed money economy to the character of modern institutions. However, "money proper" is of course an inherent part of modern social life as well as a specific type of symbolic token. It is fundamental to the disembedding of modern economic activity generally. One of the most characteristic forms of disembedding in the modern period, for instance, is the expansion of capitalistic markets (including money markets), which are from relatively early on international in scope. "Money proper" is integral to the distanciated transactions which these involve. It is also, as Simmel points out, essential to the nature of property ownership and alienability in modern economic activity.

All disembedding mechanisms, both symbolic tokens and expert systems, depend upon *trust*. Trust is therefore involved in a fundamental way with the institutions of modernity. Trust here is vested, not in individuals, but in abstract capacities. Anyone who uses monetary tokens does so on the presumption that others, whom she or he never meets, honour their value. But it is money as such which is trusted, not only, or even primarily, the persons with whom particular transactions are carried out. I shall consider the general character of trust a little later. Confining our attention for the moment to the case of money, we may note that the ties between money and trust are specifically noted and analysed by Simmel. Like Keynes he links trust in monetary transactions to "public confidence in the issuing government."

Simmel distinguishes confidence in money from the "weak inductive knowledge" involved in many forward transactions. Thus if a farmer were not confident that a field would bear grain in the following year as in previous years, she or he would not sow. Trust in money involves more than a calculation of the reliability of likely future events. Trust exists, Simmel says, when we "believe in" someone or some principle: "It expresses the feeling that there exists between our idea of a being and the being itself a definite connection and unity, a certain consistency in our conception of it, an assurance and lack of resistance in the surrender of the Ego to this conception, which may rest upon particular reasons, but is not explained by them."[24] Trust, in short, is a form of "faith," in which the confidence vested in probable outcomes expresses a commitment to something rather than just a cognitive understanding. Indeed, and I shall elaborate upon this later on, the modes of trust involved in modern institutions in the nature of the case rest upon vague and partial understandings of their "knowledge base."

Let us now look at the nature of expert systems. By expert systems I mean systems of technical accomplishment or professional expertise that organise large areas of the material and social environments in which we live today.[25] Most laypersons consult "professionals"—lawyers, architects, doctors, and so forth—only in a periodic or irregular fashion. But the systems in which the knowledge of experts is integrated influence many aspects of what we do in a *continuous* way. Simply by sitting in my house, I am involved in an expert system, or a series of such systems, in which I place my reliance. I have no particular fear in going upstairs in the dwelling, even though I know that in principle the structure might collapse. I know very little about the codes of knowledge used by the architect and the builder in the design and construction of the home, but I nonetheless have "faith" in what they have done. My "faith" is not so much in them, although I have to trust their competence, as in the authenticity of the expert knowledge which they apply—something which I cannot usually check exhaustively myself.

When I go out of the house and get into a car, I enter settings which are thoroughly permeated by expert knowledge—involving the design and construction of automobiles, highways, intersections, traffic lights, and many other items. Everyone knows that driving a car is a dangerous activity, entailing the risk of accident. In choosing to go out in the car, I accept that risk, but rely upon the aforesaid expertise to guarantee that it is minimised as far as possible. I have very little knowledge of how the car works and could only carry out minor repairs upon it myself should it go wrong. I have minimal knowledge about the technicalities of modes of road building, the maintaining of the road surfaces, or the computers which help control the movement of the traffic. When I park the car at the airport and board a plane, I enter other expert systems, of which my own technical knowledge is at best rudimentary.

Expert systems are disembedding mechanisms because, in common with symbolic tokens, they remove social relations from the immediacies of context. Both types of disembedding mechanism presume, yet also foster, the separation of time from space as the condition of the time-space distanciation which they promote. An expert system disembeds in the same way as symbolic tokens, by providing "guarantees" of expectations across distanciated time-space. This "stretching" of social systems is achieved via the impersonal nature of tests applied to evaluate technical knowledge and by public critique (upon which the production of technical knowledge is based), used to control its form.

For the lay person, to repeat, trust in expert systems depends neither upon a full initiation into these processes nor upon mastery of the knowledge they yield. Trust is inevitably in part an article of "faith." This proposition should not be oversimplified. An element of Simmel's "weak inductive knowledge" is no doubt very often present in the confidence which lay actors sustain in expert systems. There is a pragmatic element in "faith," based upon the experience that such systems generally work as they are supposed to do. In addition, there are often regulatory agencies over and above professional associations designed to protect the consumers of expert systems— bodies which licence machines, keep a watch over the standards of aircraft manufacturers, and so forth. None of this, however, alters the observation that all disembedding mechanisms imply an attitude of trust. Let me now consider how we might best understand the notion of trust and how trust connects in a general way to time-space distanciation.

Trust

The term "trust" crops up quite often in ordinary language.[26] Some senses of the term, while they share broad affinities with other usages, are relatively slight in implication. A person who says "I trust you are well" normally means little more by the polite enquiry than "I hope you are in good health"—although even here "trust" carries a somewhat stronger connotation than "hope," implying something closer to "I hope and have no reason to doubt." The attitude of confidence or reliability which enters into trust in some more significant contexts is already to be found here. When someone says, "Trust X to behave in that way," this implication is more pronounced, although not far beyond the level of "weak inductive knowledge." It is recognised that X can be relied upon to produce the behaviour in question, given appropriate circumstances. But these usages are not especially interesting for the matters at issue in the current discussion, because they do not refer to the social relations that incorporate trust. They do not relate to trust-perpetuating systems, but are designations referring to the behaviour of others; the individual involved is not called upon to display that "faith" which trust involves in its deeper meanings.

The main definition of "trust" in the *Oxford English Dictionary* describes it as "confidence in or reliance on some quality or attribute of a person or thing, or the truth of a statement," and this definition provides a useful starting point. "Confidence" and "reliance" are clearly somehow bound up with that "faith" of which, following Simmel, I have already spoken. While recognising that confidence and trust are closely allied, Luhmann makes a distinction between the two that is the basis of his work on trust.[27] Trust, he says, should be understood specifically in relation to risk, a term which only comes into being in the modern period.* The notion originated with the understanding that unanticipated results may be a consequence of our own activities or decisions, rather than expressing hidden meanings of nature or ineffable intentions of the Deity. "Risk" largely replaces what was previously thought of as *fortuna* (fortune or fate) and be-

---

*The word "risk" seems to have found its way into English in the seventeenth century and probably comes from a Spanish nautical term meaning to run into danger or to go against a rock.

---

comes separated from cosmologies. Trust presupposes awareness of circumstances of risk, whereas confidence does not. Trust and confidence both refer to expectations which can be frustrated or cast down. Confidence, as Luhmann uses it, refers to a more or less taken-for-granted attitude that familiar things will remain stable:

The normal case is that of confidence. You are confident that your expectations will not be disappointed: that politicians will try to avoid war, that cars will not break down or suddenly leave the street and hit you on your Sunday afternoon walk. You cannot live without forming expectations with respect to contingent events and you have to neglect, more or less, the possibility of disappointment. You neglect this because it is a very rare possibility, but also because you do not know what else to do. The alternative is to live in a state of permanent uncertainty and to withdraw expectations without having anything with which to replace them.[28]

Where trust is involved, in Luhmann's view, alternatives are consciously borne in mind by the individual in deciding to follow a particular course of action. Someone who buys a used car, instead of a new one, risks purchasing a dud. He or she places trust in the salesperson or the reputation of the firm to try to avoid this occurrence. Thus, an individual who does not consider alternatives is in a situation of confidence, whereas someone who does recognise those alternatives and tries to counter the risks thus acknowledged, engages in trust. In a situation of confidence, a person reacts to disappointment by blaming others; in circumstances of trust she or he must partly shoulder the blame and may regret having placed trust in someone or something. The distinction between trust and confidence depends upon whether the possibility of frustration is influenced by one's own previous behaviour and hence upon a correlate discrimination between risk and danger. Because the notion of risk is relatively recent in origin, Luhmann holds, the possibility of separating risk and danger must derive from social characteristics of modernity. Essentially, it comes from a grasp of the fact that most of the contingencies which affect human activity are humanly created, rather than merely given by God or nature.

Luhmann's approach is important and directs our attention to a number of conceptual discriminations that have to be made in understanding trust. Yet I do not think we can be content with the details of his conceptualisation. He is surely right to distinguish between trust and confidence, and between risk and danger, as well as to say that all of these are in some way closely bound up with one another. But it is unhelpful to connect the notion of trust to the specific circumstances in which individuals consciously contemplate alternative courses of action. Trust is usually much more of a continuous state than this implies. It is, I shall suggest below, a particular type of confidence rather than something distinct from it. Similar observations apply to risk and danger. I do not agree with Luhmann's statement that "if you refrain from action you run no risk"[29]—in other words, nothing ventured, nothing (potentially) lost. Inaction is often risky, and there are some risks which we all have to face whether we like it or not, such as the risks of ecological catastrophe or nuclear war. Moreover, there is no intrinsic connection between confidence and danger, even as Luhmann defines these. Danger exists in circumstances of risk and is actually relevant to defining what risk is—the risks involved in crossing the Atlantic in a small boat, for example, are considerably greater than making the journey in a large ocean liner because of the variation in the element of danger involved.

I propose to conceptualise trust and its attendant notions differently. For ease of exposition, I shall set out the elements involved as a series of ten points which include a definition of trust but also develop a range of related observations.

1. Trust is related to absence in time and in space. There would be no need to trust anyone whose activities were continually visible and whose thought processes were transparent, or to trust any system whose workings were wholly known and understood. It has been said that trust is "a device for coping with the freedom of others,"[30] but the prime condition of requirements for trust is not lack of power but lack of full information.

2. Trust is basically bound up, not with risk, but with contingency. Trust always carries the connotation of reliability in the face of contingent outcomes, whether these concern the actions of individuals or the operation of systems. In the case of trust in human agents, the presumption of reliability involves the attribution of "probity" (honour) or love. This is why trust in persons is psychologically consequential for the individual who trusts: a moral hostage to fortune is given.

3. Trust is not the same as faith in the reliability of a person or system; it is what derives from that faith. Trust is precisely the link between faith and confidence, and it is this which distinguishes it from "weak inductive knowledge." The latter is confidence based upon some sort of mastery of the circumstances in which confidence is justified. *All* trust is in a certain sense blind trust!

4. We can speak of trust in symbolic tokens or expert systems, but this rests upon faith in the correctness of

33

principles of which one is ignorant, not upon faith in the "moral uprightness" (good intentions) of others. Of course, trust in persons is always to some degree relevant to faith in systems, but concerns their *proper* working rather than their operation as such.

5. At this point we reach a definition of trust. Trust may be defined as confidence in the reliability of a person or system, regarding a given set of outcomes or events, where that confidence expresses a faith in the probity or love of another, or in the correctness of abstract principles (technical knowledge).

6. In conditions of modernity, trust exists in the context of (a) the general awareness that human activity—including within this phrase the impact of technology upon the material world—is socially created, rather than given in the nature of things or by divine influence; (b) the vastly increased transformative scope of human action, brought about by the dynamic character of modern social institutions. The concept of risk replaces that of *fortuna*, but this is not because agents in pre-modern times could not distinguish between risk and danger. Rather it represents an alteration in the perception of determination and contingency, such that human moral imperatives, natural causes, and chance reign in place of religious cosmologies. The idea of chance, in its modern senses, emerges at the same time as that of risk.

7. Danger and risk are closely related but are not the same. The difference does not depend upon whether or not an individual consciously weighs alternatives in contemplating or undertaking a particular course of action. What risk presumes is precisely danger (not necessarily awareness of danger). A person who risks something

courts danger, where danger is understood as a threat to desired outcomes. Anyone who takes a "calculated risk" is aware of the threat or threats which a specific course of action brings into play. But it is certainly possible to undertake actions or to be subject to situations which are inherently risky without the individuals involved being aware how risky they are. In other words, they are unaware of the dangers they run.

8. Risk and trust intertwine, trust normally serving to reduce or minimise the dangers to which particular types of activity are subject. There are some circumstances in which patterns of risk are institutionalised, within surrounding frameworks of trust (stock-market investment, physically dangerous sports). Here skill and chance are limiting factors upon risk, but normally risk is consciously calculated. In all trust settings, acceptable risk falls under the heading of "weak inductive knowledge," and there is virtually always a balance between trust and the calculation of risk in this sense. What is seen as "acceptable" risk—the minimising of danger—varies in different contexts, but is usually central in sustaining trust. Thus traveling by air might seem an inherently dangerous activity, given that aircraft appear to defy the laws of gravity. Those concerned with running airlines counter this by demonstrating statistically how low the risks of air travel are, as measured by the number of deaths per passenger mile.

9. Risk is not just a matter of individual action. There are "environments of risk" that collectively affect large masses of individuals—in some instances, potentially everyone on the face of the earth, as in the case of the risk of ecological disaster or nuclear war. We may define "se-

curity" as a situation in which a specific set of dangers is counteracted or minimised. The experience of security usually rests upon a balance of trust and acceptable risk. In both its factual and its experiential sense, security may refer to large aggregates or collectivities of people—up to and including global security—or to individuals.

10. The foregoing observations say nothing about what constitutes the *opposite* of trust—which is *not*, I shall argue later, simply mistrust. Nor do these points offer much concerning the conditions under which trust is generated or dissolved; I shall discuss these in some detail in later sections.

The Reflexivity of Modernity

Inherent in the idea of modernity is a contrast with tradition. As noted previously, many combinations of the modern and the traditional are to be found in concrete social settings. Indeed, some authors have argued that these are so tightly interlaced as to make any generalised comparison valueless. But such is surely not the case, as we can see by pursuing an enquiry into the relation between modernity and reflexivity.

There is a fundamental sense in which reflexivity is a defining characteristic of all human action. All human beings routinely "keep in touch" with the grounds of what they do as an integral element of doing it. I have called this elsewhere the "reflexive monitoring of action," using the phrase to draw attention to the chronic character of the processes involved.[31] Human action does not incorporate chains of aggregate interactions and reasons, but a consistent—and, as Erving Goffman above all has shown us, never-to-be-relaxed—monitoring of behaviour and its contexts. This is not the sense of reflexivity which is specifically connected with modernity, although it is the necessary basis of it.

In traditional cultures, the past is honoured and symbols are valued because they contain and perpetuate the experience of generations. Tradition is a mode of integrating the reflexive monitoring of action with the time-space organisation of the community. It is a means of handling time and space, which inserts any particular activity or experience within the continuity of past, present, and future, these in turn being structured by recurrent social practices. Tradition is not wholly static, because it has to be reinvented by each new generation as it takes over its cultural inheritance from those preceding it. Tradition does not so much resist change as pertain to a context in which there are few separated temporal and spatial markers in terms of which change can have any meaningful form.

In oral cultures, tradition is not known as such, even though these cultures are the most traditional of all. To understand tradition, as distinct from other modes of organising action and experience, demands cutting into time-space in ways which are only possible with the invention of writing. Writing expands the level of time-space distanciation and creates a perspective of past, present, and future in which the reflexive appropriation of knowledge can be set off from designated tradition. However, in pre-modern civilisations reflexivity is still largely limited to the reinterpretation and clarification of tradition, such that in the scales of time the side of the "past" is much more heavily weighed down than that of the "future." Moreover, since literacy is the monopoly of the few, the routinisation of daily life remains bound up with tradition in the old sense.

With the advent of modernity, reflexivity takes on a different character. It is introduced into the very basis of system reproduction, such that thought and action are constantly refracted back upon one another. The routinisation of daily life has no intrinsic connections with the past at all, save in so far as what "was done before" happens to coincide with what can be defended in a principled way in the light of incoming knowledge. To sanction a practice because it is traditional will not do; tradition can be justified, but only in the light of knowledge which is not itself authenticated by tradition. Combined with the inertia of habit, this means that, even in the most modernised of modern societies, tradition continues to play a role. But this role is generally much less significant than is supposed by authors who focus attention upon the integration of tradition and modernity in the contemporary world. For justified tradition is tradition in sham clothing and receives its identity only from the reflexivity of the modern.

The reflexivity of modern social life consists in the fact that social practices are constantly examined and reformed in the light of incoming information about those very practices, thus constitutively altering their character. We should be clear about the nature of this phenomenon. All forms of social life are partly constituted by actors' knowledge of them. Knowing "how to go on" in Wittgenstein's sense is intrinsic to the conventions which are drawn upon and reproduced by human activity. In all cultures, social practices are routinely altered in the light of ongoing discoveries which feed into them. But only in the era of modernity is the revision of convention radicalised to apply (in principle) to all aspects of human life, including technological intervention into the material world. It is often said that modernity is marked by an appetite for the new, but this is not perhaps completely accurate. What is characteristic of modernity is not an embracing of the new for its own sake, but the presumption of wholesale reflexivity—which of course includes reflection upon the nature of reflection itself.

Probably we are only now, in the late twentieth century, beginning to realise in a full sense how deeply unsettling this outlook is. For when the claims of reason replaced those of tradition, they appeared to offer a sense of certitude greater than that provided by preexisting dogma. But this idea only appears persuasive so long as we do not see that the reflexivity of modernity actually subverts reason, at any rate where reason is understood as the gaining of certain knowledge. Modernity is constituted in and through reflexively applied knowledge, but the equation of knowledge with certitude has turned out to be misconceived. We are abroad in a world which is thoroughly constituted through reflexively applied knowledge, but where at the same time we can never be sure that any given element of that knowledge will not be revised.

Even philosophers who most staunchly defend the claims of science to certitude, such as Karl Popper, acknowledge that, as he expresses it, "all science rests upon shifting sand."[32] In science, *nothing* is certain, and nothing can be proved, even if scientific endeavour provides us with the most dependable information about the world to which we can aspire. In the heart of the world of hard science, modernity floats free.

39

No knowledge under conditions of modernity *is* knowledge in the "old" sense, where "to know" is to be certain. This applies equally to the natural and the social sciences. In the case of social science, however, there are further considerations involved. We should recall at this point the observations made earlier about the reflexive components of sociology.

In the social sciences, to the unsettled character of all empirically based knowledge we have to add the "subversion" which comes from the reentry of social scientific discourse into the contexts it analyses. The reflection of which the social sciences are the formalised version (a specific genre of expert knowledge) is quite fundamental to the reflexivity of modernity as a whole.

Because of the close relation between the Enlightenment and advocacy of the claims of reason, natural science has usually been taken as the preeminent endeavour distinguishing the modern outlook from what went before. Even those who favour interpretative rather than naturalistic sociology have normally seen social science as the poor relation of the natural sciences, particularly given the scale of technological development consequent upon scientific discoveries. But the social sciences are actually more deeply implicated in modernity than is natural science, since the chronic revision of social practices in the light of knowledge about those practices is part of the very tissue of modern institutions.[33]

All the social sciences participate in this reflexive relation, although sociology has an especially central place. Take as an example the discourse of economics. Concepts like "capital," "investment," "markets," "industry," and many others, in their modern senses, were elaborated as part of the early development of economics as a distinct discipline in the eighteenth and early nineteenth centuries. These concepts, and empirical conclusions linked to them, were formulated in order to analyse changes involved in the emergence of modern institutions. But they could not, and did not, remain separated from the activities and events to which they related. They have become integral to what "modern economic life" actually is and inseparable from it. Modern economic activity would not be as it is were it not for the fact that all members of the population have mastered these concepts and an indefinite variety of others.

The lay individual cannot necessarily provide formal definitions of terms like "capital" or "investment," but everyone who, say, uses a savings account in a bank demonstrates an implicit and practical mastery of those notions. Concepts such as these, and the theories and empirical information linked to them, are not merely handy devices whereby agents are somehow more clearly able to understand their behaviour than they could do otherwise. They actively constitute what that behaviour is and inform the reasons for which it is undertaken. There cannot be a clear insulation between literature available to economists and that which is either read or filters through in other ways to interested parties in the population: business leaders, government officials, and members of the public. The economic environment is constantly being altered in the light of these inputs, thus creating a situation of continual mutual involvement between economic discourse and the activities to which it refers.

The pivotal position of sociology in the reflexivity of modernity comes from its role as the most generalised type of reflection upon modern social life. Let us consider an example at the "hard edge" of naturalistic sociology.

The official statistics published by governments concerning, for instance, population, marriage and divorce, crime and delinquency, and so forth, seem to provide a means of studying social life with precision. To the pioneers of naturalistic sociology, such as Durkheim, these statistics represented hard data, in terms of which the relevant aspects of modern societies can be analysed more accurately than where such figures are lacking. Yet official statistics are not just analytical characteristics of social activity, but again enter constitutively into the social universe from which they are taken or counted up. From its inception, the collation of official statistics has been constitutive of state power and of many other modes of social organisation also. The co-ordinated administrative control achieved by modern governments is inseparable from the routine monitoring of "official data" in which all contemporary states engage.

The assembling of official statistics is itself a reflexive endeavour, permeated by the very findings of the social sciences that have utilised them. The practical work of coroners, for example, is the basis for the collection of suicide statistics. In the interpretation of causes/motives for death, however, coroners are guided by concepts and theories which purport to illuminate the nature of suicide. It would not be at all unusual to find a coroner who had read Durkheim.

Nor is the reflexivity of official statistics confined to the sphere of the state. Anyone in a Western country who embarks upon marriage today, for instance, knows that divorce rates are high (and may also, however imperfectly or partially, know a great deal more about the demography of marriage and the family). Knowledge of the high rate of divorce might affect the very decision to marry, as well as decisions about related considerations—provisions about property and so forth. Awareness of levels of divorce, moreover, is normally much more than just consciousness of a brute fact. It is theorised by the lay agent in ways pervaded by sociological thinking. Thus virtually everyone contemplating marriage has some idea of how family institutions have been changing, changes in the relative social position and power of men and women, alterations in sexual mores, etc.—all of which enter into processes of further change which they reflexively inform. Marriage and the family would not be what they are today were they not thoroughly "sociologised" and "psychologised."

The discourse of sociology and the concepts, theories, and findings of the other social sciences continually "circulate in and out" of what it is that they are about. In so doing they reflexively restructure their subject matter, which itself has learned to think sociologically. *Modernity is itself deeply and intrinsically sociological.* Much that is problematic in the position of the professional sociologist, as the purveyor of expert knowledge about social life, derives from the fact that she or he is at most one step ahead of enlightened lay practitioners of the discipline.

Hence the thesis that more knowledge about social life (even if that knowledge is as well buttressed empirically as it could possibly be) equals greater control over our fate is false. It is (arguably) true about the physical world, but not about the universe of social events. Expanding our understanding of the social world might produce a progressively more illuminating grasp of human institutions and, hence, increasing "technological" control over them, if it were the case either that social life were entirely separate from human knowledge about it or that knowledge could be filtered continuously into the reasons for social action, producing step-by-step increases in the "rationality" of behaviour in relation to specific needs.

Both conditions do in fact apply to many circumstances and contexts of social activity. But each falls well short of that totalising impact which the inheritance of Enlightenment thought holds out as a goal. This is so because of the influence of four sets of factors.

One—factually very important but logically the least interesting, or at any rate the least difficult to handle analytically—is differential power. The appropriation of knowledge does not happen in a homogeneous fashion, but is often differentially available to those in power positions, who are able to place it in the service of sectional interests.

A second influence concerns the role of values. Changes in value orders are not independent of innovations in cognitive orientation created by shifting perspectives on the social world. If new knowledge could be brought to bear upon a transcendental rational basis of values, this situation would not apply. But there is no such rational basis of values, and shifts in outlook deriving from inputs of knowledge have a mobile relation to changes in value orientations.

The third factor is the impact of unintended consequences. No amount of accumulated knowledge about social life could encompass all circumstances of its implementation, even if such knowledge were wholly distinct from the environment to which it applied. If our knowledge about the social world simply got better and better, the scope of unintended consequences might become more and more confined and unwanted consequences rare. However, the reflexivity of modern social life blocks off this possibility and is itself the fourth influence involved. Although least discussed in relation to the limits of Enlightenment reason, it is certainly as significant as any of the others. The point is not that there is no stable social world to know, but that knowledge of that world contributes to its unstable or mutable character.

The reflexivity of modernity, which is directly involved with the continual generating of systematic self-knowledge, does not stabilise the relation between expert knowledge and knowledge applied in lay actions. Knowledge claimed by expert observers (in some part, and in many varying ways) rejoins its subject matter, thus (in principle, but also normally in practice) altering it. There is no parallel to this process in the natural sciences; it is not at all the same as where, in the field of microphysics, the intervention of an observer changes what is being studied.

Modernity or Post-Modernity?

At this point we can connect the discussion of reflexivity with the debates about post-modernity. "Post-modernity" is often used as if it were synonymous with post-modernism, post-industrial society, etc. Although the idea of post-industrial society, as worked out by Daniel Bell at any rate,[34] is well explicated, the other two concepts mentioned above certainly are not. I shall draw a distinction between them here. Post-modernism, if it means anything, is best kept to refer to styles or movements within literature, painting, the plastic arts, and architecture. It concerns aspects of *aesthetic reflection* upon the nature of modernity. Although sometimes only rather

45

vaguely designated, modernism is or was a distinguishable outlook in these various areas and might be said to have been displaced by other currents of a post-modernist variety. (A separate work could be written on this issue, which I shall not analyse here.)

Post-modernity refers to something different, at least as I shall define the notion. If we are moving into a phase of post-modernity, this means that the trajectory of social development is taking us away from the institutions of modernity towards a new and distinct type of social order. Post-modernism, if it exists in cogent form, might express an awareness of such a transition but does not show that it exists.

What does post-modernity ordinarily refer to? Apart from the general sense of living through a period of marked disparity from the past, the term usually means one or more of the following: that we have discovered that nothing can be known with any certainty, since all pre-existing "foundations" of epistemology have been shown to be unreliable; that "history" is devoid of teleology and consequently no version of "progress" can plausibly be defended; and that a new social and political agenda has come into being with the increasing prominence of ecological concerns and perhaps of new social movements generally. Scarcely anyone today seems to identify post-modernity with what it was once widely accepted to mean—the replacement of capitalism by socialism. Pushing this transition away from centre stage, in fact, is one of the main factors that has prompted current discussions about the possible dissolution of modernity, given Marx's totalising view of history.

Let us first of all dismiss as unworthy of serious intellectual consideration the idea that no systematic knowledge of human action or trends of social development is possible. Were anyone to hold such a view (and if indeed it is not inchoate in the first place), they could scarcely write a book about it. The only possibility would be to repudiate intellectual activity altogether—even "playful deconstruction"—in favour, say, of healthy physical exercise. Whatever the absence of foundationalism in epistemology implies, it is not this. For a more plausible starting point, we might look to the "nihilism" of Nietzsche and Heidegger. In spite of the differences between the two philosophers, there is a view upon which they converge. Both link with modernity the idea that "history" can be identified as a progressive appropriation of rational foundations of knowledge. According to them, this is expressed in the notion of "overcoming": the formation of new understandings serves to identify what is of value, and what is not, in the cumulative stock of knowledge.[35] Each finds it necessary to distance himself from the foundational claims of the Enlightenment yet cannot criticise these from the vantage point of superior or better-founded claims. They therefore abandon the notion of "critical overcoming" so central to the Enlightenment critique of dogma.

Anyone who sees in this a basic transition from modernity to post-modernity, however, faces great difficulties. One of the main objections is obvious and well known. To speak of post-modernity as superseding modernity appears to invoke that very thing which is declared (now) to be impossible: giving some coherence to history and pinpointing our place in it. Moreover, if Nietzsche was the principal author disconnecting post-modernity from modernity, a phenomenon supposedly happening today, how is it possible that he saw all this

47

almost a century ago? Why was Nietzsche able to make such a breakthrough without, as he freely said, doing anything more than uncovering the hidden presuppositions of the Enlightenment itself?

It is difficult to resist the conclusion that the break with foundationalism is a significant divide in philosophical thought, having its origins in the mid- to late nineteenth century. But it surely makes sense to see this as "modernity coming to understand itself" rather than the overcoming of modernity as such.[36] We can interpret this in terms of what I shall label *providential* outlooks. Enlightenment thought, and Western culture in general, emerged from a religious context which emphasised teleology and the achievement of God's grace. Divine providence had long been a guiding idea of Christian thought. Without these preceding orientations, the Enlightenment would scarcely have been possible in the first place. It is in no way surprising that the advocacy of unfettered reason only reshaped the ideas of the providential, rather than displacing it. One type of certainty (divine law) was replaced by another (the certainty of our senses, of empirical observation), and divine providence was replaced by providential progress. Moreover, the providential idea of reason coincided with the rise of European dominance over the rest of the world. The growth of European power provided, as it were, the material support for the assumption that the new outlook on the world was founded on a firm base which both provided security and offered emancipation from the dogma of tradition.

Yet the seeds of nihilism were there in Enlightenment thought from the beginning. If the sphere of reason is wholly unfettered, no knowledge can rest upon an unquestioned foundation, because even the most firmly held notions can only be regarded as valid "in principle" or "until further notice." Otherwise they would relapse into dogma and become separate from the very sphere of reason which determines what validity is in the first place. Although most regarded the evidence of our senses as the most dependable information we can obtain, even the early Enlightenment thinkers were well aware that such "evidence" is always in principle suspect. Sense data could never provide a wholly secure base for knowledge claims. Given the greater awareness today that sensory observation is permeated by theoretical categories, philosophical thought has in the main veered quite sharply away from empiricism. Moreover, since Nietzsche we are much more clearly aware of the circularity of reason, as well as the problematic relations between knowledge and power.

Rather than these developments taking us "beyond modernity," they provide a fuller understanding of the reflexivity inherent in modernity itself. Modernity is not only unsettling because of the circularity of reason, but because the nature of that circularity is ultimately puzzling. How can we justify a commitment to reason in the name of reason? Paradoxically, it was the logical positivists who stumbled across this issue most directly, as a result of the very lengths to which they went to strip away all residues of tradition and dogma from rational thought. Modernity turns out to be enigmatic at its core, and there seems no way in which this enigma can be "overcome." We are left with questions where once there appeared to be answers, and I shall argue subsequently that it is not only philosophers who realise this. A general awareness of the phenomenon filters into anxieties which press in on everyone.

Post-modernity has been associated not only with the end of foundationalism but with the "end of history." Since I have referred to it earlier, there is no need to provide a detailed discussion of this notion here. "History" has no intrinsic form and no overall teleology. A plurality of histories can be written, and they cannot be anchored by reference to an Archimedean point (such as the idea that history has an evolutionary direction). History must not be equated with "historicity," since the second of these is distinctively bound up with the institutions of modernity. Marx's historical materialism mistakenly identifies the one with the other and thereby not only attributes a false unity to historical development but also fails adequately to discern the special qualities of modernity. The points at issue here were well covered in the celebrated debate between Lévi-Strauss and Sartre.[37] The "use of history to make history" is substantially a phenomenon of modernity and not a generalised principle that can be applied to all eras—it is one version of modernity's reflexivity. Even history as dating, the charting of sequences of changes between dates, is a specific way of coding temporality.

We must be careful how we understand historicity. It might be defined as the use of the past to help shape the present, but it does not depend upon respect for the past. On the contrary, historicity means the use of knowledge about the past as a means of breaking with it—or, at any rate, only sustaining what can be justified in a principled manner.[38] Historicity in fact orients us primarily towards the future. The future is regarded as essentially open, yet as counterfactually conditional upon courses of action undertaken with future possibilities in mind. This is a fundamental aspect of the time-space "stretch" which conditions of modernity make both possible and necessary. "Futurology"—the charting of possible/likely/available futures—becomes more important than charting out the past. Each of the types of disembedding mechanism mentioned previously presumes a future orientation of this sort. The break with providential views of history, the dissolution of foundationalism, together with the emergence of counterfactual future-oriented thought and the "emptying out" of progress by continuous change, are so different from the core perspectives of the Enlightenment as to warrant the view that far-reaching transitions have occurred. Yet referring to these as post-modernity is a mistake which hampers an accurate understanding of their nature and implications. The disjunctions which have taken place should rather be seen as resulting from the self-clarification of modern thought, as the remnants of tradition and providential outlooks are cleared away. We have not moved beyond modernity but are living precisely through a phase of its radicalisation.

The gradual decline in European or Western global hegemony, the other side of which is the increasing expansion of modern institutions worldwide, is plainly one of the main influences involved here. The projected "decline of the West," of course, has been a preoccupation among some authors since the latter part of the nineteenth century. As used in such a context, the phrase usually referred to a cyclical conception of historical change, in which modern civilisation is simply seen as one regionally located civilisation among others which have preceded it in other areas of the world. Civilisations have their periods of youth, maturity, and old age, and as they are replaced by others, the regional distribution of global power alters. But modernity is *not* just one civilisation among others, according to the discontinuist interpretation I have suggested above. The declining grip of the West over the rest of the world is not a result of the diminishing impact of the institutions which first arose there but, on the contrary, a result of their global spread. The economic, political, and military power which gave the West its primacy, and which was founded upon the conjunction of the four institutional dimensions of modernity I shall shortly discuss, no longer so distinctly differentiates the Western countries from others elsewhere. We can interpret this process as one of *globalisation*, a term which must have a key position in the lexicon of the social sciences.

What of the other sets of changes often linked, in some sense or another, to post-modernity: the rise of new social movements and the creation of novel political agendas? These are indeed important, as I shall try to show later. However, we have to sort our way circumspectly through the various theories or interpretations that have been advanced on the basis of them. I shall analyse post-modernity as a series of immanent transitions away from—or "beyond"—the various institutional clusters of modernity that will be distinguished subsequently. We do not yet live in a post-modern social universe, but we can still see more than a few glimpses of the emergence of ways of life and forms of social organisation which diverge from those fostered by modern institutions.

In terms of this analysis, it can easily be seen why the radicalising of modernity is so unsettling, and so significant. Its most conspicuous features—the *dissolution of evolutionism*, the *disappearance of historical teleology*, the recognition of *thoroughgoing, constitutive reflexivity*, together with the *evaporating of the privileged posi-*

tion of the West—move us into a new and disturbing universe of experience. If the "us" here still refers primarily to those living in the West itself—or, more accurately, the industrialised sectors of the world—it is something whose implications are felt everywhere.

Summary

We are now in a position to sum up the discussion thus far. Three dominant sources of the dynamism of modernity have been distinguished, each connected with the other:

The separation of time and space. This is the condition of time-space distanciation of indefinite scope; it provides means of precise temporal and spatial zoning.

The development of disembedding mechanisms. These "lift out" social activity from localised contexts, reorganising social relations across large time-space distances.

The reflexive appropriation of knowledge. The production of systematic knowledge about social life becomes integral to system reproduction, rolling social life away from the fixities of tradition.

Taken together, these three features of modern institutions help to explain why living in the modern world is more like being aboard a careering juggernaut (an image I shall develop in more detail later) rather than being in a carefully controlled and well-driven motor car. The reflexive appropriation of knowledge, which is intrinsically energising but also necessarily unstable, extends to incorporate massive spans of time-space. The disembedding mechanisms provide the means of this extension by lifting social relations out of their "situatedness" in specific locales.

The disembedding mechanisms can be represented as follows:

Symbolic tokens and *expert systems* involve *trust*, as distinct from confidence based on weak inductive knowledge.

Trust operates in environments of risk, in which varying levels of security (protection against dangers) can be achieved.

The relation between trust and disembedding remains abstract here. We have to investigate later how trust, risk, security, and danger articulate in conditions of modernity. We also have to consider circumstances in which trust lapses and how situations of absence of trust might best be understood.

Knowledge (which should usually be understood here as "claims to knowledge") reflexively applied to social activity is filtered by four sets of factors:

Differential power. Some individuals or groups are more readily able to appropriate specialised knowledge than others.

The role of values. Values and empirical knowledge are connected in a network of mutual influence.

The impact of unintended consequences. Knowledge about social life transcends the intentions of those who apply it to transformative ends.

The circulating of social knowledge in the double hermeneutic. Knowledge reflexively applied to the conditions of system reproduction intrinsically alters the circumstances to which it originally referred.

Subsequently we shall trace out the implications of these features of reflexivity for the environments of trust and risk found in the contemporary social world.

II

The Institutional Dimensions of Modernity

Earlier I mentioned the tendency of most sociological perspectives or theories to look for a single dominant institutional nexus in modern societies: are modern institutions capitalistic, or are they industrial? This long-term debate is by no means devoid of significance today. Nonetheless, it is based in some part upon mistaken premises, since in each case a certain reductionism is involved—either industrialism is seen as a subtype of capitalism or vice versa. In contrast to such reductionism, we should see capitalism and industrialism as two distinct "organisational clusters" or dimensions involved in the institutions of modernity. I shall define them here as follows.

Capitalism is a system of commodity production, centred upon the relation between private ownership of capital and propertyless wage labour, this relation forming the main axis of a class system. Capitalist enterprise depends upon production for competitive markets, prices being signals for investors, producers, and consumers alike.

The chief characteristic of *industrialism* is the use of

inanimate sources of material power in the production of goods, coupled to the central role of machinery in the production process. A "machine" can be defined as an artifact that accomplishes set tasks by employing such power sources as the means of its operation. Industrialism presupposes the regularised social organisation of production in order to coordinate human activity, machines, and the inputs and outputs of raw materials and goods. Industrialism should not be understood in too narrow a sense—as its origin in the "Industrial Revolution" tempts us to do. That phrase conjures up an imagery of coal and steam power and of large, heavy machinery clanking away in grubby workshops and factories. No less than to such situations, the notion of industrialism applies to high-technology settings where electricity is the only power source, and where electronic microcircuits are the only mechanised devices. Industrialism, moreover, affects not only the workplace but transportation, communication, and domestic life.

We can recognise *capitalist societies* as one distinct subtype of modern societies in general. A capitalist society is a system having a number of specific institutional features. First, its economic order involves the characteristics noted above. The strongly competitive and expansionist nature of capitalist enterprise means that technological innovation tends to be constant and pervasive. Second, the economy is fairly distinct, or "insulated," from other social arenas, particularly political institutions. Given the high rates of innovation in the economic sphere, economic relationships have considerable sway over other institutions. Third, the insulation of polity and economy (which may take many varying forms) is founded upon the preeminence of private property in the means of production. (Private property here does not necessarily refer to individual entrepreneurship, but to the widespread private ownership of investments.) The ownership of capital is directly bound up with the phenomenon of "propertylessness"—the commodification of wage labour—in the class system. Fourth, the autonomy of the state is conditioned, although not in any strong sense determined, by its reliance upon capital accumulation, over which its control is far less than complete.

But why is capitalist society a society at all? This question is left unanswered if we simply characterise the capitalist social order in terms of its main institutional alignments. For, given its expansionist characteristics, capitalistic economic life is only in a few respects confined to the boundaries of specific social systems. From its early origins capitalism is international in scope. A capitalist society is a "society" only because it is a nation-state. The characteristics of the nation-state in some substantial part must be explained and analysed separately from discussion of the nature of either capitalism or industrialism. The administrative system of the capitalist state, and of modern states in general, has to be interpreted in terms of the coordinated control over delimited territorial arenas which it achieves. As was mentioned earlier, no premodern states were able even to approach the level of administrative coordination developed in the nation-state.

Such administrative concentration depends in turn upon the development of *surveillance* capacities well beyond those characteristic of traditional civilisations, and the apparatuses of surveillance constitute a third institutional dimension associated, like capitalism and industrialism, with the rise of modernity. Surveillance refers to the supervision of the activities of subject populations in the political sphere—although its importance as a basis of administrative power is by no means confined to that sphere. Supervision may be direct (as in many of the instances discussed by Foucault, such as prisons, schools, or open workplaces),[39] but more characteristically it is indirect and based upon the control of information.

There is a fourth institutional dimension to be distinguished: *control of the means of violence*. Military power was always a central feature of pre-modern civilisations. Yet in those civilisations the political centre was never able for long to secure stable military support and typically fell short of securing a monopoly control of the means of violence within its territories. The military strength of the ruling authorities depended upon alliances with local princes or warlords, who were always liable either to break away from or directly to challenge the ruling groups. The successful monopoly of the means of violence within territorially precise borders is distinctive to the modern state. So also is the existence of specific links to industrialism, permeating both the organisation of the military and the weaponry at their disposal. The "industrialisation of war" radically changes the character of warfare, ushering in an era of "total war" and later the nuclear age.

Clausewitz was the classic interpreter of the relation between war and the nation-state in the nineteenth century, but in fact his views were already substantially obsolete when he developed them. War, for Clausewitz, was diplomacy by other means: it was what is used when ordinary negotiation or other modes of persuasion or coercion fail in the relations between states.[40] Total war blunts

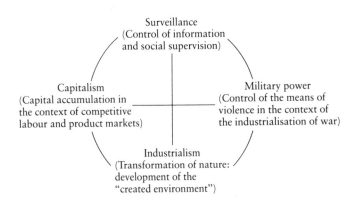

Surveillance
(Control of information
and social supervision)

Capitalism
(Capital accumulation in
the context of competitive
labour and product markets)

Military power
(Control of the means of
violence in the context of
the industrialisation of war)

Industrialism
(Transformation of nature:
development of the
"created environment")

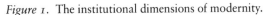

Figure 1. The institutional dimensions of modernity.

the use of war as a political instrument, since the sufferings inflicted on both sides tend to far outweigh whatever diplomatic gains may be achieved through it. The possibility of nuclear war makes this obvious.

The four basic institutional dimensions of modernity and their interrelations can be set out as in Figure 1.

To begin on the left of the circle, capitalism involves the insulation of the economic from the political against the backdrop of competitive labour and product markets. Surveillance, in turn, is fundamental to all the types of organisation associated with the rise of modernity, in particular the nation-state, which has historically been intertwined with capitalism in their mutual development. Similarly, there are close substantive connections between the surveillance operations of nation-states and the altered nature of military power in the modern period. The successful monopoly of the means of violence on the part of the modern state rests upon the secular maintenance of new codes of criminal law, plus the supervisory control of "deviance." The military becomes a relatively remote backup to the internal hegemony of the civil authorities, and the armed forces for the most part "point outwards" towards other states.

Moving further around the circle, there are direct relations between military power and industrialism, one main expression of which is the industrialisation of war. Similarly, clear connections may be established between industrialism and capitalism—connections which are fairly familiar and well documented, in spite of the priority dispute about their interpretation noted earlier. Industrialism becomes the main axis of the interaction of human beings with nature in conditions of modernity. In most pre-modern cultures, even in the large civilisations, humans mostly saw themselves as continuous with nature. Their lives were tied up with nature's moods and vagaries—the availability of natural sources of sustenance, the flourishing or otherwise of crops and pastoral animals, and the impact of natural disasters. Modern industry, shaped by the alliance of science and technology, transforms the world of nature in ways unimaginable to earlier generations. In the industrialised sectors of the globe—and, increasingly, elsewhere—human beings live in a *created environment*, an environment of action which is, of course, physical but no longer just natural. Not just the built environment of urban areas but most other landscapes as well become subject to human co-ordination and control.

The straight lines in the figure indicate further connections which can be analysed. For example, surveillance has been quite closely involved with the development of industrialism, consolidating administrative power within plants, factories, and workshops. Rather than pursuing such considerations, however, I shall turn to look briefly—very briefly, given the huge subject matter involved—at how the different institutional clusters were bound up with one another in the development of modern institutions.

Capitalistic enterprise, we can agree with Marx, played a major part in levering modern social life away from the institutions of the traditional world. Capitalism is inherently highly dynamic because of the connections established between competitive economic enterprise and generalised processes of commodification. For reasons diagnosed by Marx, the capitalist economy, both internally and externally (within and outside the purview of the nation-state), is intrinsically unstable and restless. All economic reproduction in capitalism is "expanded reproduction," because the economic order cannot remain in a more or less static equilibrium, as was the case in most traditional systems. The emergence of capitalism, as Marx says, preceded the development of industrialism and indeed provided much of the impetus to its emergence. Industrial production and the associated constant revolutionising of technology make for more efficient and cheaper production processes. The commodification of labour power was a particularly important point of linkage between capitalism and industrialism, because "abstract labour" can be directly programmed into the technological design of production.

The development of abstract labour power also formed a major point of connection between capitalism, industrialism, and the changing nature of control of the means of violence. Marx's writings are again useful for analysing this, although he did not develop them explicitly in the direction called for.[41] In pre-modern states, class systems were rarely wholly economic: exploitative class relations were in some part sustained by force or the threat of its use. The dominant class was able to deploy such force through direct access to the means of violence—it was often a class of warriors. With the emergence of capitalism, the nature of class domination became substantially different. The capitalistic labour contract, a focal point of the newly emergent class system, involved the hiring of abstract labour, rather than the servitude of the "whole person" (slavery), a proportion of the working week (corvée labour), or of produce (tithes or taxation in kind). The capitalist labour contract does not rest upon the direct possession of the means of violence, and wage labour is nominally free. Class relations thus became incorporated directly within the framework of capitalist production, rather than being open and sanctioned by violence. This process occurred in historical conjunction with the monopolising of control of the means of violence in the hands of the state. Violence, as it were, was "extruded" from the labour contract and concentrated in the hands of the state authorities.

If capitalism was one of the great institutional elements promoting the acceleration and expansion of modern institutions, the other was the nation-state. Nation-states, and the nation-state system, cannot be explained in terms of the rise of capitalistic enterprise, however convergent the interests of states and capitalistic prosperity have sometimes been. The nation-state system was forged by myriad contingent events from the loosely scattered order of post-feudal kingdoms and principalities whose existence distinguished Europe from centralised agrarian empires. The spread of modern institutions across the world was originally a Western phenomenon and was affected by all four institutional dimensions mentioned above.

Nation-states concentrated administrative power far more effectively than traditional states were able to do, and consequently even quite small states could mobilise social and economic resources beyond those available to pre-modern systems. Capitalist production, especially when conjoined to industrialism, provided a massive leap forward in economic wealth and also in military power. The combination of all these factors made Western expansion seemingly irresistible.

Behind these institutional clusterings lie the three sources of the dynamism of modernity distinguished earlier: time-space distanciation, disembedding, and reflexivity. These are not, as such, types of institution, but rather facilitating conditions for the historical transitions referred to in the preceding paragraphs. Without them, the tearing away of modernity from traditional orders could not have happened in so radical a way, so rapidly, or across such a worldwide stage. They are involved in, as well as conditioned by, the institutional dimensions of modernity.

The Globalising of Modernity

Modernity is inherently globalising—this is evident in some of the most basic characteristics of modern institutions, including particularly their disembeddedness and reflexivity. But what exactly is globalisation, and how might we best conceptualise the phenomenon? I shall consider these questions at some length here, since the central importance of globalising processes today has scarcely been matched by extended discussions of the concept in the sociological literature. We can begin by recalling some points made earlier. The undue reliance which sociologists have placed upon the idea of "society," where this means a bounded system, should be replaced by a starting point that concentrates upon analysing how social life is ordered across time and space—the problematic of time-space distanciation. The conceptual framework of time-space distanciation directs our attention to the complex relations between *local involvements* (circumstances of co-presence) and *interaction across distance* (the connections of presence and absence). In the modern era, the level of time-space distanciation is much higher than in any previous period, and the relations between local and distant social forms and events become correspondingly "stretched." Globalisation refers essentially to that stretching process, in so far as the modes of connection between different social contexts or regions become networked across the earth's surface as a whole.

Globalisation can thus be defined as the intensification of worldwide social relations which link distant localities in such a way that local happenings are shaped by events occurring many miles away and vice versa. This is a dialectical process because such local happenings may move in an obverse direction from the very distanciated relations that shape them. *Local transformation* is as much a part of globalisation as the lateral extension of social connections across time and space. Thus whoever studies cities today, in any part of the world, is aware that what happens in a local neighbourhood is likely to be influenced by factors—such as world money and commodity markets—operating at an indefinite distance away from that neighbourhood itself. The outcome is not necessarily, or even usually, a generalised set of changes acting in a uniform direction, but consists in mutually opposed tendencies. The increasing prosperity of an urban area in Singapore might be causally related, via a complicated network of global economic ties, to the impoverishment of a neighbourhood in Pittsburgh whose local products are uncompetitive in world markets.

Another example from the very many that could be offered is the rise of local nationalisms in Europe and elsewhere. The development of globalised social relations probably serves to diminish some aspects of nationalist feeling linked to nation-states (or some states) but may be causally involved with the intensifying of more localised nationalist sentiments. In circumstances of accelerating globalisation, the nation-state has become "too small for the big problems of life, and too big for the small problems of life."[42] At the same time as social relations become laterally stretched and as part of the same process, we see the strengthening of pressures for local autonomy and regional cultural identity.

Two Theoretical Perspectives

Apart from the work of Marshall McLuhan and a few other individual authors, discussions of globalisation tend to appear in two bodies of literature, which are largely distinct from one another. One is the literature of international relations, the other that of "world-system theory," particularly as associated with Immanuel Wallerstein, which stands fairly close to a Marxist position.

Theorists of international relations characteristically focus upon the development of the nation-state system, analysing its origins in Europe and its subsequent worldwide spread. Nation-states are treated as actors, engaging with one another in the international arena—and with other organisations of a transnational kind (intergovernmental organisations or non-state actors). Although various theoretical positions are represented in this literature, most authors paint a rather similar picture in analysing the growth of globalisation.[43] Sovereign states, it is presumed, first emerge largely as separate entities, having more or less complete administrative control within their borders. As the European state system matures and later becomes a global nation-state system, patterns of interdependence become increasingly developed. These are not only expressed in the ties states form with one another in the international arena, but in the burgeoning of intergovernmental organisations. These processes mark an overall movement towards "one world," although they are continually fractured by war. Nation-states, it is held, are becoming progressively less sovereign than they used to be in terms of control over their own affairs—although few today anticipate in the near future the emergence of the "world-state" which many in the early part of this century foresaw as a real prospect.

While this view is not altogether wrong, some major reservations have to be expressed. For one thing, it again covers only one overall dimension of globalisation as I wish to utilise the concept here—the international coordination of states. Regarding states as actors has its uses and makes sense in some contexts. However, most theorists of international relations do not explain *why* this usage makes sense; for it does so only in the case of nation-states, not in that of pre-modern states. The reason has to do with a theme discussed earlier—there is a far greater concentration of administrative power in nation-states than in their precursors, in which it would be relatively meaningless to speak of "governments" who negotiate with other "governments" in the name of their respective nations. Moreover, treating states as actors having connections with each other and with other organisations in the international arena makes it difficult to deal with social relations that are not between or outside states, but simply crosscut state divisions.

A further shortcoming of this type of approach concerns its portrayal of the increasing unification of the nation-state system. The sovereign power of modern states was not formed prior to their involvement in the nation-state system, even in the European state system, but developed in conjunction with it. Indeed, the sovereignty of the modern state was from the first *dependent upon the relations between states*, in terms of which each state (in principle if by no means always in practice) recognised the autonomy of others within their own borders. No state, however powerful, held as much sovereign control in practice as was enshrined in legal principle. The history of the past two centuries is thus not one of the progressive loss of sovereignty on the part of the nation-state. Here again we must recognise the dialectical character of globalisation and also the influence of processes of uneven development. Loss of autonomy on the part of some states or groups of states has often gone along with an *increase* in that of others, as a result of alliances, wars, or political and economic changes of various sorts. For instance, although the sovereign control of some of the "classical" Western nations may have diminished as a result of the acceleration of the global division of labour over the past thirty years, that of some Far Eastern countries—in some respects at least—has grown.

Since the stance of world-system theory differs so much from international relations, it is not surprising to find that the two literatures are at arm's distance from one another. Wallerstein's account of the world system makes many contributions, in both theory and empirical analysis.[44] Not least important is the fact that he skirts the sociologists' usual preoccupation with "societies" in favour of a much more embracing conception of globalised relationships. He also makes a clear differentiation between the modern era and preceding ages in terms of the phenomena with which he is concerned. What he refers to as "world economies"—networks of economic connections of a geographically extensive sort—have existed prior to modern times, but these were notably different from the world system that has developed over the past three or four centuries. Earlier world economies were usually centred upon large imperial states and never covered more than certain regions in which the power of these states was concentrated. The emergence of capitalism, as Wallerstein analyses it, ushers in a quite different type of order, for the first time genuinely global in its span and based more on economic than political power—the "world capitalist economy." The world capitalist economy, which has its origins in the sixteenth and seventeenth centuries, is integrated through commercial and manufacturing connections, not by a political centre. Indeed, there exists a multiplicity of political centres, the nation-states. The modern world system is divided into three components, the core, the semi-periphery, and the periphery, although where these are located regionally shifts over time.

According to Wallerstein, the worldwide reach of capitalism was established quite early on in the modern period: "Capitalism was from the beginning an affair of the world economy and not of nation-states. . . . Capital has never allowed its aspirations to be determined by national boundaries."[45] Capitalism has been such a fundamental globalising influence precisely because it is an economic rather than a political order; it has been able to penetrate far-flung areas of the world which the states of its origin could not have brought wholly under their political sway. The colonial administration of distant lands may in some situations have helped to consolidate economic expansion, but it was never the main basis of the spread of capitalistic enterprise globally. In the late twentieth century, where colonialism in its original form has all but disappeared, the world capitalist economy continues to involve massive imbalances between core, semi-periphery, and periphery.

Wallerstein successfully breaks away from some of the limitations of much orthodox sociological thought, most notably the strongly defined tendency to focus upon "endogenous models" of social change. But his work has its own shortcomings. He continues to see only one dominant institutional nexus (capitalism) as responsible for modern transformations. World-system theory thus concentrates heavily upon economic influences and finds it difficult satisfactorily to account for just those phenomena made central by the theorists of international relations: the rise of the nation-state and the nation-state system. Moreover, the distinctions between core, semi-periphery, and periphery (themselves perhaps of questionable value), based upon economic criteria, do not allow us to illuminate political or military concentrations of power, which do not align in an exact way to economic differentiations.

Dimensions of Globalisation

I shall, in contrast, regard the world capitalist economy as one of four dimensions of globalisation, following the four-fold classification of the institutions of modernity mentioned above (see Figure 2).[46] The nation-state system is a second dimension; as the discussion above indicated, although these are connected in various ways, neither can be explained exhaustively in terms of the other.

If we consider the present day, in what sense can world economic organisation be said to be dominated by capitalistic economic mechanisms? A number of considerations are relevant to answering this question. The main centres of power in the world economy are capitalist states—states in which capitalist economic enterprise (with the class relations that this implies) is the chief form of production. The domestic and international economic policies of these states involve many forms of regulation of economic activity, but, as noted, their institutional organisation maintains an "insulation" of the economic from the political. This allows wide scope for the global activities of business corporations, which always have a home base within a particular state but may develop many other regional involvements elsewhere.

Business firms, especially the transnational corporations, may wield immense economic power, and have the capacity to influence political policies in their home bases and elsewhere. The biggest transnational companies today have budgets larger than those of all but a few nations. But there are some key respects in which their power cannot rival that of states—especially important here are the factors of territoriality and control of the

Figure 2. The dimensions of globalisation.

means of violence. There is no area on the earth's surface, with the partial exception of the polar regions, which is not claimed as the legitimate sphere of control of one state or another. All modern states have a more or less successful monopoly of control of the means of violence within their own territories. No matter how great their economic power, industrial corporations are not military organisations (as some of them were during the colonial period), and they cannot establish themselves as political/legal entities which rule a given territorial area.

If nation-states are the principal "actors" within the global political order, corporations are the dominant agents within the world economy. In their trading relations with one another, and with states and consumers, companies (manufacturing corporations, financial firms, and banks) depend upon production for profit. Hence the spread of their influence brings in its train a global extension of commodity markets, including money markets. However, even in its beginnings, the capitalist world economy was never just a market for the trading of goods

71

and services. It involved, and involves today, the commodifying of labour power in class relations which separate workers from control of their means of production. This process, of course, is fraught with implications for global inequalities.

All nation-states, capitalist and state socialist, within the "developed" sectors of the world, are primarily reliant upon industrial production for the generation of the wealth upon which their tax revenues are based. The socialist countries form something of an enclave within the capitalist world economy as a whole, industry being more directly subject to political imperatives. These states are scarcely post-capitalist, but the influence of capitalistic markets upon the distribution of goods and labour power is substantially muted. The pursuit of growth by both Western and East European societies inevitably pushes economic interests to the forefront of the policies which states pursue in the international arena. But it is surely plain to all, save those under the sway of historical materialism, that the material involvements of nation-states are not governed purely by economic considerations, real or perceived. The influence of any particular state within the global political order is strongly conditioned by the level of its wealth (and the connection between this and military strength). However, states derive their power from their sovereign capabilities, as Hans J. Morgenthau emphasises.[47] They do not operate as economic machines, but as "actors" jealous of their territorial rights, concerned with the fostering of national cultures, and having strategic geopolitical involvements with other states or alliances of states.

The nation-state system has long participated in that reflexivity characteristic of modernity as a whole. The very existence of sovereignty should be understood as something that is reflexively monitored, for reasons already indicated. Sovereignty is linked to the replacement of "frontiers" by "borders" in the early development of the nation-state system: autonomy inside the territory claimed by the state is sanctioned by the recognition of borders by other states. As noted, this is one of the major factors distinguishing the nation-state system from systems of states in the pre-modern era, where few reflexively ordered relations of this kind existed and where the notion of "international relations" made no sense.

One aspect of the dialectical nature of globalisation is the "push and pull" between tendencies towards centralisation inherent in the reflexivity of the system of states on the one hand and the sovereignty of particular states on the other. Thus, concerted action between countries in some respects diminishes the individual sovereignty of the nations involved, yet by combining their power in other ways, it increases their influence within the state system. The same is true of the early congresses which, in conjunction with war, defined and redefined states' borders—and of truly global agencies such as the United Nations. The global influence of the U.N. (still decisively limited by the fact that it is not territorial and does not have significant access to the means of violence) is not purchased solely by means of a diminution of the sovereignty of nation-states—things are more complicated than this. An obvious example is that of the "new nations"—autonomous nation-states set up in erstwhile colonised areas. Armed struggle against the colonising countries was very generally a major factor in persuading the colonisers to retreat. But discussion in the U.N. played a key role in setting up ex-colonial areas as states with internationally recognised borders. However weak some of the new nations may be economically and militarily, their emergence *as* nation-states (or, in many cases, "state-nations") marks a net gain in terms of sovereignty, as compared to their previous circumstances.

The third dimension of globalisation is the world military order. In specifying its nature, we have to analyse the connections between the industrialisation of war, the flow of weaponry and techniques of military organisation from some parts of the world to others, and the alliances which states build with one another. Military alliances do not necessarily compromise the monopoly over the means of violence held by a state within its territories, although in some circumstances they certainly can do so.

In tracing the overlaps between military power and the sovereignty of states, we find the same push-and-pull between opposing tendencies noted previously. In the current period, the two most militarily developed states, the United States and the Soviet Union, have built a bipolar system of military alliances of truly global scope. The countries involved in these alliances necessarily accept limitations over their opportunities to forge independent military strategies externally. They may also forfeit complete monopoly of military control within their own territories, in so far as American or Soviet forces stationed there take their orders from abroad. Yet, as a result of the massive destructive power of modern weaponry, almost all states possess military strength far in excess of that of even the largest of pre-modern civilisations. Many economically weak Third World countries are militarily powerful. In an important sense there is no "Third World" in respect of weaponry, only a "First World," since most countries maintain stocks of technologically advanced armaments and have modernised the military in a thoroughgoing way. Even the possession of nuclear weaponry is not confined to the economically advanced states.

The globalising of military power obviously is not confined to weaponry and alliances between the armed forces of different states—it also concerns war itself. Two world wars attest to the way in which local conflicts became matters of global involvement. In both wars, the participants were drawn from virtually all regions (although the Second World War was a more truly worldwide phenomenon). In an era of nuclear weaponry, the industrialisation of war has proceeded to a point at which, as was mentioned earlier, the obsolescence of Clausewitz's main doctrine has become apparent to everyone.[48] The only point of holding nuclear weapons—apart from their possible symbolic value in world politics—is to deter others from using them.

While this situation may lead to a suspension of war between the nuclear powers (or so we all must hope), it scarcely prevents them from engaging in military adventures outside their own territorial domains. The two superpowers in particular engage in what might be called "orchestrated wars" in peripheral areas of military strength. By these I mean military encounters, with the governments of other states or with guerilla movements or both, in which the troops of the superpower are not necessarily even engaged at all, but where that power is a prime organising influence.

The fourth dimension of globalisation concerns industrial development. The most obvious aspect of this is the expansion of the global division of labour, which includes the differentiations between more and less industrialised areas in the world. Modern industry is intrinsically based on divisions of labour, not only on the level of job tasks but on that of regional specialisation in terms of type of industry, skills, and the production of raw materials. There has undoubtedly taken place a major expansion of global interdependence in the division of labour since the Second World War. This has helped to bring about shifts in the worldwide distribution of production, including the deindustrialisation of some regions in the developed countries and the emergence of the "Newly Industrialising Countries" in the Third World. It has also undoubtedly served to reduce the internal economic hegemony of many states, particularly those with a high level of industrialisation. It is more difficult for the capitalist countries to manage their economies than formerly was the case, given accelerating global economic interdependence. This is almost certainly one of the major reasons for the declining impact of Keynesian economic policies, as applied at the level of the national economy, in current times.

One of the main features of the globalising implications of industrialism is the worldwide diffusion of machine technologies. The impact of industrialism is plainly not limited to the sphere of production, but affects many aspects of day-to-day life, as well as influencing the generic character of human interaction with the material environment.

Even in states which remain primarily agricultural, modern technology is often applied in such a way as to alter substantially preexisting relations between human social organisation and the environment. This is true, for example, of the use of fertilisers or other artificial farming methods, the introduction of modern farming machinery, and so forth. The diffusion of industrialism has created "one world" in a more negative and threatening sense than that just mentioned—a world in which there are actual or potential ecological changes of a harmful sort that affect everyone on the planet. Yet industrialism has also decisively conditioned our very sense of living in "one world." For one of the most important effects of industrialism has been the transformation of technologies of communication.

This comment leads on to a further and quite fundamental aspect of globalisation, which lies behind each of the various institutional dimensions that have been mentioned and which might be referred to as cultural globalisation. Mechanised technologies of communication have dramatically influenced all aspects of globalisation since the first introduction of mechanical printing into Europe. They form an essential element of the reflexivity of modernity and of the discontinuities which have torn the modern away from the traditional.

The globalising impact of media was noted by numerous authors during the period of the early growth of mass circulation newspapers. Thus one commentator in 1892 wrote that, as a result of modern newspapers, the inhabitant of a local village has a broader understanding of contemporary events than the prime minister of a hundred years before. The villager who reads a paper "interests himself simultaneously in the issue of a revolution in Chile, a bush-war in East Africa, a massacre in North China, a famine in Russia."[49]

The point here is not that people are contingently aware of many events, from all over the world, of which previously they would have remained ignorant. It is that the global extension of the institutions of modernity would be impossible were it not for the pooling of knowledge which is represented by the "news." This is perhaps less obvious on the level of general cultural awareness than in more specific contexts. For example, the global money markets of today involve direct and simultaneous access to pooled information on the part of individuals spatially widely separated from one another.

III

___

In conditions of modernity, larger and larger numbers of
people live in circumstances in which disembedded institutions, linking local practices with globalised social relations, organise major aspects of day-to-day life. In the
following sections of this study, I want to look more
closely at how the sustaining of trust connects with these
phenomena, as well as broaching questions of security,
risk, and danger in the modern world. I have previously
related trust, in an abstract way, to time-space distanciation, but we now have to consider the substance of trust
relations in conditions of modernity. If the immediate
bearing of globalisation upon this discussion is not immediately apparent, I hope it will become so later.

To proceed further, we need to make some conceptual
distinctions over and above those already formulated.

Trust and Modernity

First, I want to complement the notion of disembedding with one of *reembedding*. By this I mean the reappropriation or recasting of disembedded social relations
so as to pin them down (however partially or transitorily)

to local conditions of time and place. I want also to distinguish between what I shall call *facework commitments* and *faceless commitments*. The former refers to trust relations which are sustained by or expressed in social connections established in circumstances of copresence. The second concerns the development of faith in symbolic tokens or expert systems, which, taken together, I shall term *abstract systems*. My overall theses will be that all disembedding mechanisms interact with reembedded contexts of action, which may act either to support or to undermine them; and that faceless commitments are similarly linked in an ambiguous way with those demanding facework.

We can find a starting point for this discussion in the familiar sociological observation that in modern social life many people, much of the time, interact with others who are strangers to them. As Simmel pointed out, the meaning of the term "stranger" changes with the coming of modernity.[50] In pre-modern cultures, where the local community always remains the basis of wider social organisation, the "stranger" refers to a "whole person"— someone who comes from the outside and who is potentially suspect. There may be many respects in which a person moving into a small community from elsewhere fails to receive the trust of the insiders, even perhaps after having lived in that community for many years. In modern societies, by contrast, we do not characteristically interact with strangers as "whole people" in the same way. Particularly in many urban settings, we interact more or less continuously with others whom we either do not know well or have never met before—but this interaction takes the form of relatively fleeting contacts.

The variety of encounters that make up day-to-day life

in the anonymous settings of modern social activity are sustained in the first instance by what Goffman has called "civil inattention."[51] This phenomenon demands complex and skilled management on the part of those who exhibit it, even though it may seem to involve the most minor cues and signals. Two people approach and pass one another on a city sidewalk. What could be more trivial and uninteresting? Such an event may happen millions of times a day even within a single urban area. Yet something is going on here which links apparently minor aspects of bodily management to some of the most pervasive features of modernity. The "inattention" displayed is not indifference. Rather it is a carefully monitored demonstration of what might be called polite estrangement. As the two people approach one another, each rapidly scans the face of the other, looking away as they pass— Goffman calls this a mutual "dimming of the lights." The glance accords recognition of the other as an agent and as a potential acquaintance. Holding the gaze of the other only briefly, then looking ahead as each passes the other couples such an attitude with an implicit reassurance of lack of hostile intent.

The maintenance of civil inattention seems to be a very general presupposition of the trust presumed in regular encounters with strangers in public places. How important this is can easily be seen in circumstances where it is absent or fractured. The "hate stare," for instance, which, as Goffman notes, whites in the southern United States have been known in the past to give to blacks in public settings reflects a rejection of the rights of blacks to participate in some orthodox forms of day-to-day interaction with whites. In a somewhat contrary example, a person walking through a tough neighbourhood may walk fast, looking straight ahead the whole time, or furtively, in both cases avoiding any eye contact with other passersby. A lack of elementary trust in the possible intentions of others leads the individual to avoid catching their gaze, which might precipitate a potentially hostile engagement.

Civil inattention is the most basic type of facework commitment involved in encounters with strangers in circumstances of modernity. It involves not just the use of the face itself, but the subtle employment of bodily posture and positioning which gives off the message "you may trust me to be without hostile intent"—in the street, public buildings, trains or buses, or at ceremonial gatherings, parties, or other assemblies. Civil inattention is trust as "background noise"—not as a random collection of sounds, but as carefully restrained and controlled social rhythms. It is characteristic of what Goffman calls "unfocused interaction."

The mechanisms of "focused interaction," or encounters, are quite different. Encounters, whether with strangers, acquaintances, or intimates, also involve generalised practices connected with the sustaining of trust. The transition from civil inattention to the opening of an encounter, as Goffman points out, is fraught with adverse possibilities for each individual concerned. The elementary trust which any initiation of an encounter presumes tends to be sanctioned by a perception of "established trustworthiness" and/or by the maintenance of informal rituals—again, often of a complex kind. Encounters with strangers or acquaintances—people whom an individual has met before, but does not know well—balance trust, tact, and power. Tact and rituals of politeness are mutual protective devices, which strangers or acquaintances knowingly use (mostly on the level of practical consciousness) as a kind of implicit social contact. Differential power, particularly where it is very marked, can breach or skew norms of tact and politeness rituals—as can the familiarity of established trustworthiness between friends and intimates.

Trust in Abstract Systems

Much more could be said on the subject of the interweaving of trust, tact, and power in encounters with nonintimates, but at this point I want to concentrate upon *trustworthiness*, particularly in relation to symbolic tokens and expert systems. Trustworthiness is of two sorts. There is that established between individuals who are well known to one another and who, on the basis of long-term acquaintance, have substantiated the credentials which render each reliable in the eyes of the other. Trustworthiness in respect of the disembedding mechanisms is different, although reliability is still central and credentials are certainly involved. In some circumstances, trust in abstract systems does not presuppose any encounters at all with the individuals or groups who are in some way "responsible" for them. But in the large majority of instances such individuals or groups are involved, and I shall refer to encounters with them on the part of lay actors as the *access points* of abstract systems. The access points of abstract systems are the meeting ground of facework and faceless commitments.

It will be a basic part of my argument that *the nature of modern institutions is deeply bound up with the mechanisms of trust in abstract systems*, especially trust in expert systems. In conditions of modernity, the future is always open, not just in terms of the ordinary contingency of things, but in terms of the reflexivity of knowledge in relation to which social practices are organised. This counterfactual, future-oriented character of modernity is largely structured by trust vested in abstract systems—which by its very nature is filtered by the trustworthiness of established expertise. It is extremely important to be clear about what this involves. The reliance placed by lay actors upon expert systems is not just a matter—as was normally the case in the pre-modern world—of generating a sense of security about an independently given universe of events. It is a matter of the calculation of benefit and risk in circumstances where expert knowledge does not just provide that calculus but actually *creates* (or reproduces) the universe of events, as a result of the continual reflexive implementation of that very knowledge.

One of the things this means, in a situation in which many aspects of modernity have become globalised, is that no one can completely opt out of the abstract systems involved in modern institutions. This is most obviously the case in respect of such phenomena as the risk of nuclear war or of ecological catastrophe. But it is true in a more thoroughgoing way of large tracts of day-to-day life, as it is lived by most of the population. Individuals in pre-modern settings, in principle and in practice, could ignore the pronouncements of priests, sages, and sorcerers and get on with the routines of daily activity. But this is not the case in the modern world, in respect of expert knowledge.

For this reason, contacts with experts or their representatives or delegates, in the shape of encounters at access points, are peculiarly consequential in modern societies. That this is so is very generally recognised both by lay individuals and by the operators or purveyors of abstract systems. Various considerations typically are involved here. Encounters with the representatives of abstract systems, of course, can be regularised and may easily take on characteristics of trustworthiness associated with friendship and intimacy. This may be the case, for example, with a doctor, dentist, or travel agent dealt with regularly over a period of years. However, many encounters with the representatives of abstract systems are more periodic or transitory than this. Irregular encounters are probably those in which the evidential criteria of reliability have to be especially carefully laid out and protected, although such criteria are also displayed in the whole range of lay-professional encounters.

At access points the facework commitments which tie lay actors into trust relations ordinarily involve displays of manifest trustworthiness and integrity, coupled with an attitude of "business-as-usual," or unflappability. Although everyone is aware that the real repository of trust is in the abstract system, rather than the individuals who in specific contexts "represent" it, access points carry a reminder that it is flesh-and-blood people (who are potentially fallible) who are its operators. Facework commitments tend to be heavily dependent upon what might be called the *demeanour* of system representatives or operators. The grave deliberations of the judge, solemn professionalism of the doctor, or stereotyped cheerfulness of the air cabin crew all fall into this category. It is understood by all parties that reassurance is called for, and reassurance of a double sort: in the reliability of the specific individuals involved and in the (necessarily arcane) knowledge or skills to which the lay individual has no effective access. An attitude of business-as-usual is likely to be particularly important where the dangers involved are open to view, rather than forming a basis of purely counterfactual risks. To pursue the air travel example, the studied casualness and calm cheer of air crew personnel are probably as important in reassuring passengers as any number of announcements demonstrating statistically how safe air travel is.

It is virtually always the case that at access points a strict division is made, to use two more of Goffman's concepts, between "frontstage" and "backstage" performances. We do not need a functionalist "explanation" to see why this is so. Control of the threshold between the front- and backstage is part of the essence of professionalism. Why do experts keep concealed from others a good deal of what they do? One reason is quite straightforward: the exercise of expertise often requires specialised environments, as well as concerted mental concentration, which would be difficult to achieve in public view. But there are other reasons. There is a difference between expertise and the expert, which those who work at access points ordinarily wish to minimise as far as possible. Experts can get things wrong, by misinterpreting or being ignorant of expertise they are presumed to possess.

The clear distinction of front- and backstage reinforces demeanour as a means of reducing the impact of imperfect skills and human fallibility. Patients are not likely to trust medical staff so implicitly if they have full knowledge of the mistakes which are made in the wards and on the operating table. A further reason concerns the areas of contingency that always remain in the workings of abstract systems. There is no skill so carefully honed and no form of expert knowledge so comprehensive that elements of hazard or luck do not come into play. Experts ordinarily presume that lay individuals will feel more reassured if they are not able to observe how frequently these elements enter into expert performance.

Trust mechanisms do not relate only to the connections between lay persons and experts: they are also bound up with the activities of those who are "within" abstract systems. Codes of professional ethics, in some cases backed by legal sanctions, form one means whereby the trustworthiness of colleagues or associates is internally managed. Yet even for those who might seem most intrinsically committed to the abstract systems they sustain, facework commitments are generally important as a mode of generating continuing trustworthiness. This forms one type of example of the reembedding of social relations. Reembedding here represents a means of anchoring trust in the trustworthiness and integrity of colleagues. As Deirdre Boden expresses this:

The businessman who says, "When are you going to be in New York?" or the lunches of show biz types on Sunset Boulevard or the academics who cross continents to read dense fifteen-minute papers in windowless air-conditioned rooms aren't concerned with tourist or culinary or scholarly activities. They need, like soldiers of old, to see the whites of the eyes of colleagues and enemies alike, to reaffirm and, more centrally, update the basis of trust.[52]

Reembedding in such contexts, as the quotation indicates, connects confidence in abstract systems to their reflexively mobile nature, as well as providing encounters and rituals which sustain collegial trustworthiness.

We can represent these points in summary form as follows:

Trust relations are basic to the extended time-space distanciation associated with modernity.

Trust in systems takes the form of *faceless commitments*, in which faith is sustained in the workings of knowledge of which the lay person is largely ignorant.

Trust in persons involves *facework commitments*, in which indicators of the integrity of others (within given arenas of action) are sought.

Reembedding refers to processes by means of which faceless commitments are sustained or transformed by facework.

Civil inattention is a fundamental aspect of trust relations in the large-scale, anonymous settings of modernity. It is the reassuring "noise" in the backdrop of the formation and dissolution of encounters, which involve their own specific trust mechanisms, that is, facework commitments.

Access points are points of connection between lay individuals or collectivities and the representatives of abstract systems. They are places of vulnerability for abstract systems, but also junctions at which trust can be maintained or built up.

Trust and Expertise

The observations made so far in this section all bear more upon how trust is managed in relation to abstract systems, rather than answering the question: why *do* most people, most of the time, trust in practices and social mechanisms about which their own technical knowledge is slight or nonexistent? The query can be answered in various ways. We know enough about the reluctance with which, in the early phase of modern social development, populations adapted to new social practices—such as the introduction of professionalised forms of medicine—to recognise the importance of socialisation in relation to such trust. The influence of the "hidden curriculum" in processes of formal education is probably decisive here. What is conveyed to the child in the teaching of science is not just the content of technical findings but, more important for general social attitudes, an aura of respect for technical knowledge of all kinds. In most modern educational systems, the teaching of science always starts from "first principles," knowledge regarded as more or less indubitable. Only if someone stays with science training for some while is she or he likely to be introduced to contentious issues or to become fully aware of the potential fallibility of all claims to knowledge in science.

Science has thus long maintained an image of reliable knowledge which spills over into an attitude of respect for most forms of technical specialism. However, at the same time, lay attitudes to science and to technical knowledge generally are typically ambivalent. This is an ambivalence that lies at the core of all trust relations, whether it be trust in abstract systems or in individuals. For trust is only demanded where there is ignorance— either of the knowledge claims of technical experts or of the thoughts and intentions of intimates upon whom a person relies. Yet ignorance always provides grounds for scepticism or at least caution. Popular representations of science and technical expertise typically bracket respect with attitudes of hostility or fear, as in the stereotypes of the "boffin," a humourless technician with little understanding of ordinary people, or the mad scientist. Professions whose claim to specialist knowledge is seen mainly as a closed shop, having an insider's terminology seemingly invented to baffle the layperson—like lawyers or sociologists—are likely to be seen with a particularly jaundiced eye.

Respect for technical knowledge usually exists in conjunction with a pragmatic attitude towards abstract systems, based upon attitudes of scepticism or reserve. Many people, as it were, make a "bargain with modernity" in terms of the trust they vest in symbolic tokens and expert systems. The nature of the bargain is governed by specific admixtures of deference and scepticism, comfort and fear. Though we cannot escape the impact of modern institutions altogether, within the broad scope of attitudes of pragmatic acceptance many possible orientations can exist (or coexist, in true ambivalence). An individual may choose to move to a different area, for example, rather than drink fluoridated water, or drink bottled water rather than use that from the tap. It would be an extreme attitude, however, to refuse to use piped water altogether.

Trust is different from "weak inductive knowledge," but the faith it involves does not always presume a conscious act of commitment. In conditions of modernity, attitudes of trust towards abstract systems are usually routinely incorporated into the continuity of day-to-day activities and are to a large extent enforced by the intrinsic circumstances of daily life. Thus trust is much less of a "leap to commitment" than a tacit acceptance of circumstances in which other alternatives are largely foreclosed. Still, it would be quite mistaken to see this situation as just a sort of passive dependence, reluctantly conceded—a point I shall develop further below.

Attitudes of trust, or lack of trust, toward specific abstract systems are liable to be strongly influenced by experiences at access points—as well as, of course, by updates of knowledge which, via the communications media and other sources, are provided for laypersons as well as for technical experts. The fact that access points are places of tension between lay scepticism and professional expertise makes them acknowledged sources of vulnerability for abstract systems. In some cases, a person who has unfortunate experiences at a given access point, where the technical skills in question are relatively low-level, may decide to opt out of the client-layperson relationship. Thus someone who finds that the "experts" she employs consistently fail to fix the central heating properly may decide to fix it herself by learning the basic principles involved. In other instances bad experiences at access points may lead either to a sort of resigned cynicism or, where this is possible, to disengagement from the system altogether.* An individual who invests in certain shares on the advice of a stockbroker and who loses money might decide to hold money in a credit account instead. That person might even resolve to hold assets only in gold in the future. But once again, it would be very difficult to disengage from the monetary system com-

---

*Modern government depends upon a complex series of trust relations between political leaders and the populace. Electoral systems might be regarded not just as means of securing interest representation, but as ways of institutionalising access points connecting politicians and the mass of the population. Election manifestos and other propaganda are methods of demonstrating trustworthiness, and a good deal of reembedding usually occurs—babies are beamed at, and hands are shaken. Trust in political expertise is a topic in its own right; but since this is one area of trust relations which has quite often been analysed, I shall not discuss it in detail here. One should note, however, that disengagement from governmental systems is today well-nigh impossible, given the global spread of nation-states. One may be able to leave a country where government policies are particularly oppressive or distasteful, but only by entering the territory of another state and becoming subject to its jurisdiction.

pletely, and this could only be done if the individual were to try to live in self-sufficient poverty.

Before considering more directly the circumstances in which trust is built up or forfeited, we have to complement the preceding discussion with an analysis of trust in persons rather than in systems. This brings us to issues to do with the psychology of trust.

Trust and Ontological Security

There are some aspects of trust and processes of personality development which seem to apply in all cultures, pre-modern and modern. I shall not attempt to provide an extensive coverage of these, but will concentrate upon the connections between trust and *ontological security*. Ontological security is one form, but a very important form, of feelings of security in the wide sense in which I have used the term earlier.[53] The phrase refers to the confidence that most humans beings have in the continuity of their self-identity and in the constancy of the surrounding social and material environments of action. A sense of the reliability of persons and things, so central to the notion of trust, is basic to feelings of ontological security; hence the two are psychologically closely related.

Ontological security has to do with "being" or, in the terms of phenomenology, "being-in-the-world." But it is an emotional, rather than a cognitive, phenomenon, and it is rooted in the unconscious. Philosophers have shown us that on a cognitive level there are few, if any, aspects of our personal existence about which we can be certain. This is perhaps part of the reflexivity of modernity, but is certainly not limited in its application only to a specific historical period. Certain questions—"Do I really exist?"

"Am I the same person today as I was yesterday?" "Do other people really exist?" "Does what I see in front of me continue to be there when I turn my back on it?"—cannot be answered in an indubitable way by rational argument.

Philosophers pose questions about the nature of being, but they are not, we may suppose, ontologically insecure in their ordinary actions, and in this outlook they are in accord with the mass of the population. The same is not true of a minority of people who treat our inability to be certain about such matters not just as an intellectual worry, but as a deep disquiet that feeds into many of the things that they do. A person who is existentially unsure about whether he or she is several selves, or whether others really exist, or whether what is perceived really exists, may be entirely incapable of inhabiting the same social universe as other human beings. Certain categories of individuals regarded by others as mentally ill, particularly schizophrenics, do think and act in this way.[54]

Whatever else such schizophrenic behaviour shows, however, it is hardly expressive of a mental lack—as is also true of many kinds of anxiety states, in crippling or milder versions. Suppose someone anguishes constantly, in a deep-seated way, about whether others harbour malicious intentions towards him or her. Or suppose a person worries constantly about the possibility of nuclear war and cannot push the thought of this risk aside. While "normal" individuals may regard such anxieties, when they are profound and chronic, as irrational, these feelings are more the result of emotional supersensitivity than irrationality. For the risk of nuclear war *is* always there as an immanent possibility in today's world; and, since no individual ever has direct access to the thoughts of another, no one *can* be absolutely sure, in a logical rather than an emotional sense, that malicious ideas are not constantly in the minds of others with whom she or he interacts.

Why is everyone not always in a state of high ontological insecurity, given the enormity of such potential existential troubles? The origins of the security that the majority feel, most of the time, in relation to these possible self-interrogations are to be found in certain characteristic experiences of early childhood. "Normal" individuals, I want to argue, receive a basic "dosage" of trust in early life that deadens or blunts these existential susceptibilities. Or, to alter the metaphor slightly, they receive an emotional inoculation which protects against the ontological anxieties to which all human beings are potentially subject. The agent of this inoculation is the primary caretaking figure of infancy: for the vast majority of individuals, the mother.

The work of Erik Erikson provides a major source of insights into the significance of trust in the context of early child development. What Erikson calls "basic trust," he shows, is at the heart of a lasting ego-identity. In discussing trust in infancy, Erikson draws attention to just that necessary element of faith to which I have already alluded.

While some psychologists have spoken of the development of "confidence" in infancy, he says, he prefers the word "trust" because there is "more naïveté" to it. Moreover, he adds, trust implies not only "that one has learned to rely on the sameness and continuity of the outer providers" but also "that one may trust oneself." Trust in others is developed in conjunction with the formation of an inner sense of trustworthiness, which provides a basis of a stable self-identity subsequently.

Hence very early on trust implies a *mutuality* of experience. The infant learns to rely upon the consistency and attention of its providers. But at the same time it learns that it must cope with its own urges in ways deemed satisfactory by them, and that the caretakers expect reliability or trustworthiness in the child's own behaviour. Infantile schizophrenia, Erikson points out, gives graphic evidence of what can happen if basic trust is not established between the child and its providers. The infant develops little sense of the "reality" of things or of other people, because the regular nourishment of affection and caring is lacking. Bizarre behaviour and withdrawal represent attempts to cope with an indeterminate or actively hostile environment in which the absence of feelings of inner trustworthiness mirror the unreliability of the outside world.

A faith in the caretaker's love is the essence of that leap to commitment which basic trust—and all forms of trust thereafter—presumes.

[Parents] create a sense of trust in their children by that kind of administration which in its quality combines sensitive care of the baby's individual needs and a firm sense of personal trustworthiness within the trusted framework of their culture's life style. This forms the basis in the child for a sense of identity which will later combine a sense of being "all right", of being oneself, and of becoming what other people trust one will become. . . . Parents must not only have certain ways of guiding by prohibition and permission; they must also be able to represent to the child a deep, an almost somatic conviction that there is a meaning to what they are doing. Ultimately, children become neurotic not from frustrations, but from the lack or loss of societal meaning in those frustrations.

But, even under the most favourable circumstances, this stage seems to introduce psychic life (and become prototypical for) a sense of inner division and universal nostalgia for a paradise forfeited. It is against this powerful combination of a sense of having been deprived, of having been divided, and of having been abandoned that basic trust must maintain itself throughout life.[55]

These insights, by no means peculiar to Erikson, form a general emphasis of the object-relations school of psychoanalytic thought.* Some very comparable ideas were developed earlier by D. W. Winnicott. It is not the satisfaction of organic drives, he says, which causes an infant "to begin to be, to feel that life is real, to find life worth living." Such an orientation derives instead from the relation between the baby and its caretaker and is dependent upon what Winnicott calls the "potential space" between them. Potential space is the separateness which is created between infant and caretaker—an autonomy of action and an emergent sense of identity and of "the reality of things"—and derives from the baby's trust in the reliability of the parental figure. Potential space is something of a misnomer because, as Winnicott makes clear, it refers to the capacity of the infant to tolerate the caretaker being away in time as well as in space.[56]

*The ideas of the object-relations school are more appropriate to the arguments developed here than those found in the Lacanian psychoanalysis which is more influential today in some areas of social theory. Lacan's work is significant because it helps capture the fragility and fragmentation of the self. In so doing, however—in common with post-structuralist thought in general—it focuses primarily upon one type of process, which is in actuality complemented by countertendencies towards integration and wholeness. Object-relations theory is informative because it analyses how the individual obtains a sense of coherence and how this connects with reassurance in the "reality" of the external world. In my view, such an approach is (or can be made) consonant with a Wittgensteinian view of the "givenness" of the world of objects and events, which can be "experienced" only as it is lived in and which is intrinsically refractory to being put into words.

Crucial to the intersection of trust with emergent social capabilities on the part of the infant, therefore, is *absence*. Here, at the heart of the psychological development of trust, we rediscover the problematic of time-space distanciation. For a fundamental feature of the early formation of trust is trust in the caretaker's return. A feeling of the reliability, yet independent experience, of others—central to a sense of continuity of self-identity—is predicated upon the recognition that the absence of the mother does not represent a withdrawal of love. Trust thus brackets distance in time and space and so blocks off existential anxieties which, if they were allowed to concretise, might become a source of continuing emotional and behavioural anguish throughout life.

Erving Goffman expresses this with his usual pungency when (in the context of a discussion of risk) he remarks that

poets and the religious are wont to argue that if an individual compares the very considerable time he is slated to spend dead with the relatively brief time allowed him to strut and fret in this world, he might well find reason for viewing all of his life as a very fateful play of very short span, every second of which should fill him with anxiety about what is used up. And in truth, our rather brief time *is* ticking away, but we seem only to hold our breath for seconds and minutes of it.[57]

Trust, ontological security, and a feeling of the continuity of things and persons remain closely bound up with one another in the adult personality. Trust in the reliability of nonhuman objects, it follows from this analysis, is based upon a more primitive faith in the reliability and nurturance of human individuals. Trust in others is a psychological need of a persistent and recurrent kind. Drawing assurance from the reliability or integrity of others is a sort of emotional regrooving which accompanies the experience of familiar social and material environments. Ontological security and routine are intimately connected, via the pervasive influence of habit. The infant's early caretakers normally place an overriding importance upon the following of routines, a matter of both intense frustration and reward for the infant. The predictability of the (apparently) minor routines of day-to-day life is deeply involved with a sense of psychological security. When such routines are shattered—for whatever reason—anxieties come flooding in, and even very firmly founded aspects of the personality of the individual may become stripped away and altered.[58]

Attachment to routine is always ambivalent, this being an expression of those feelings of loss which, as Erikson notes, are inevitably a part of basic trust. Routine is psychologically relaxing, but in an important sense it is not something anyone can ever be relaxed *about*. The continuity of the routines of daily life is achieved only through the constant vigilance of the parties involved—although it is almost always accomplished at the level of practical consciousness. Demonstration of this continual renewal of the "contract" which individuals undertake with one another is exactly the point of Harold Garfinkel's "experiments with trust."[59] These experiments provide graphic illustration of the emotionally disturbing impact of disregarding even apparently inconsequential features of ordinary talk. The result is a suspension of trust in the other as a reliable, competent agent, and a flooding-in of existential anxiety that takes the form of feelings of hurt, puzzlement, and betrayal, together with suspicion and hostility.

This work and that of others upon the minutiae of everyday talk and interaction strongly suggest that what is learned in the formation of basic trust is not just the correlation of routine, integrity, and reward. What is also mastered is an extremely sophisticated methodology of practical consciousness, which is a continuing protective device (although fraught with possibilities of fracture and disjunction) against the anxieties which even the most casual encounter with others can potentially provoke. We have already noted civil inattention as one general way in which trust is "done" as a feature of copresence outside of focused encounters. In facework engagements themselves, the sustaining of basic trust is accomplished through the chronic monitoring of the gaze, bodily posture, and gesture, and the conventions of orthodox conversation.

The analysis developed in this section provides the opportunity to sketch in the answer to a question which was left open before: what is the opposite of trust? Obviously there are circumstances where the absence of trust could be adequately characterised as mistrust, either in respect of abstract systems or persons. The term "mistrust" applies most easily when we are speaking of the relation of an agent to a specific system, individual, or type of individual. In respect of abstract systems, mistrust means being sceptical about, or having an actively negative attitude toward, the claims to expertise that system incorporates. In the case of persons, it means doubting or disbelieving the claims to integrity their actions embody or display. However, "mistrust" is too weak a term to express the antithesis of *basic* trust, the focal element in a generalised set of relations to the social and physical environment. The forging of trust here is the very condition of acknowledging the clear identity of objects and persons. If basic trust is not developed or its inherent ambivalence not contained, the outcome is persistent existential anxiety. In its most profound sense, the antithesis of trust is thus a state of mind which could best be summed up as existential *angst* or *dread*.

The Pre-Modern and the Modern

If there are features of the psychology of trust which are universal, or near-universal, there are also fundamental contrasts between the conditions of trust relations in pre-modern cultures and those of the modern world. It is not only trust that we have to consider here, but broad aspects of the connections between trust and risk, and between security and danger. It is a risky business in itself to draw generalised contrasts between the modern era and the whole gamut of pre-modern social orders. The abruptness and extent of the discontinuities between modernity and pre-modern institutions, however, justifies the attempt, although inevitably over-simplifications are involved. Table 1 provides an overall orientation to the distinctions I want to make between environments of trust and of risk.

In all pre-modern cultures, including the large agrarian civilisations, for reasons already discussed, the level of time-space distanciation is relatively low as compared with conditions of modernity. Ontological security in the pre-modern world has to be understood primarily in relation to contexts of trust, and forms of risk or danger, anchored in the local circumstances of place. Because of its inherent connection with absence, trust is always bound up with modes of organising "reliable" interactions across time-space.

Four localised contexts of trust tend to predominate in pre-modern cultures, although each of these has many variations according to the particular social order in question. The first context of trust is the kinship system, which in most pre-modern settings provides a relatively stable mode of organising "bundles" of social relations across time and space. Kinship connections are often a focus of tension and conflict. But however many conflicts they involve and anxieties they provoke, they are very generally bonds which can be relied upon in the structuring of actions in fields of time-space. This is true on the level of both fairly impersonal and more personal connections. In other words, kinspeople can usually be relied upon to meet a range of obligations more or less regardless of whether they feel personally sympathetic towards the specific individuals involved. Moreover, kinship often does provide a stabilising network of amicable or intimate relations which endure across time-space. Kinship, in sum, provides a nexus of reliable social connections which, in principle and very commonly in practice, form an organising medium of trust relations.

Much the same can be said of the local community. We should avoid the romanticised view of community which has often surfaced in social analysis when traditional cultures are compared to the modern. I mean here to stress the importance of *localised relations* organised in terms of *place*, where place has not yet become transformed by distanciated time-space relations. In the large majority of pre-modern settings, including most cities, the local milieu is the site of clusters of interweaving social relations, the low spatial span of which provides for their solidity

TABLE I
Environments of Trust and Risk
in Pre-Modern and Modern Cultures

	PRE-MODERN	MODERN
	General context: overriding importance of localised trust	*General context:* trust relations vested in disembedded abstract systems
ENVIRONMENT OF TRUST	1. *Kinship relations* as an organising device for stabilising social ties across time-space	1. *Personal relationships* of friendship or sexual intimacy as means of stabilising social ties
	2. *The local community* as a *place*, providing a familiar milieu	2. *Abstract systems* as a means of stabilising relations across indefinite spans of time-space
	3. *Religious cosmologies* as modes of belief and ritual practice providing a providential interpretation of human life and of nature	3. *Future-oriented*, counter-factual thought as a mode of connecting past and present
	4. *Tradition* as a means of connecting present and future; past-oriented in reversible time	
ENVIRONMENT OF RISK	1. Threats and dangers emanating from *nature*, such as the prevalence of infectious diseases, climatic unreliability, floods, or other natural disasters	1. Threats and dangers emanating from the *reflexivity* of modernity
	2. The threat of *human violence* from marauding armies, local warlords, brigands, or robbers	2. The threat of *human violence* from the industrialisation of war
	3. Risk of a *fall from religious grace* or of malicious magical influence	3. The threat of *personal meaninglessness* deriving from the reflexivity of modernity as applied to the self

in time. Migrations of population, nomadism, and the long-distance journeys of merchants and adventurers were common enough in pre-modern times. But the large majority of the population were relatively immobile and isolated, as compared to the regular and dense forms of mobility (and awareness of other ways of life) provided for by modern means of transportation. The locality in pre-modern contexts is the focus of, and contributes to, ontological security in ways that are substantially dissolved in circumstances of modernity.

A third influence is that of religious cosmology. Religious beliefs can be a source of extreme anxiety or despair—so much so that they must be included as one of the main parameters of (experienced) risk and danger in many pre-modern settings. But in other respects religious cosmologies provide moral and practical interpretations of personal and social life, as well as of the natural world, which represent an environment of security for the believer. The Christian deity commands us, "Trust in me, for I am the one true God." While most religions are not so monotheistic, the idea of reliance upon supernatural beings or forces is a common feature of many otherwise different religious beliefs. Religion is an organising medium of trust in more than one way. Not only deities and religious forces provide providentially dependable supports: so also do religious functionaries. Most important of all, religious beliefs typically inject reliability into the experience of events and situations and form a framework in terms of which these can be explained and responded to.

As with the other contexts of trust in pre-modern orders, I place the emphasis here upon religion as something that generates a sense of the reliability of social and natural events, and thus contributes to the bracketing of time-space. It is possible that religion is connected psychologically to trust mechanisms in terms of the personages and forces it represents, in such a way that these are directly expressive of trust—or its absence—in parental figures. Certainly Freud suggested as much,[60] and many other authors influenced by psychoanalysis have agreed. Erikson is a case in point: the "faith" which trust presupposes and which first of all is vested in the infant's caretakers, he says, has its "institutional safeguard" in organised religion.

Trust born of care is, in fact, the touchstone of the *actuality* of a given religion. All religions have in common the periodical childlike surrender to a provider or providers who dispense earthly fortune as well as spiritual health . . . [and] the insight that individual trust must become a common faith, individual mistrust a commonly formulated evil, while the individual's restoration must become part of the ritual practice of many, and must become a sign of trustworthiness in the community.[61]

Even given the extraordinary diversity of the world's religions, it is difficult to resist the conclusion that there must be some element of validity in this view; however, the standpoint I wish to develop here does not depend primarily upon it.

The fourth main context of trust relations in premodern cultures is tradition itself. Tradition, unlike religion, does not refer to any particular body of beliefs and practices, but to the manner in which those beliefs and practices are organised, especially in relation to time. Tradition reflects a distinct mode of structuring temporality (which also has direct implications for action across space). Lévi-Strauss's notion of "reversible time" is central to understanding the temporality of traditional beliefs and activities. Reversible time is the temporality of repetition and is governed by the logic of repetition—the past is a means of organising the future. The orientation to the past which is characteristic of tradition does not differ from the outlook of modernity only in being backward-looking rather than forward-looking; this is in fact too crude a way to express the contrast. Rather, neither "the past" nor "the future" is a discrete phenomenon, separated from the "continuous present," as in the case of the modern outlook. Past time is incorporated into present practices, such that the horizon of the future curves back to intersect with what went before.

Tradition is routine. But it is routine which is intrinsically meaningful, rather than merely empty habit for habit's sake. Time and space are not the contentless dimensions they become with the development of modernity but are contextually implicated in the nature of lived activities. The meanings of routine activities lie in the general respect or even reverence intrinsic to tradition and in the connection of tradition with ritual. Ritual often has a compulsive aspect to it, but it is also deeply comforting, for it infuses a given set of practices with a sacramental quality. Tradition, in sum, contributes in basic fashion to ontological security in so far as it sustains trust in the continuity of past, present, and future, and connects such trust to routinised social practices.

To specify these various contexts of trust in premodern cultures is not to say that traditional settings were comforting and psychologically snug, while modern ones are not. There are some definite respects in which levels of ontological insecurity are higher in the modern world than in most circumstances of pre-modern social life, for reasons I shall try to identify. Yet the settings of traditional cultures were in a generic way fraught with anxieties and uncertainties. I refer to these, taken together, as the environment of risk characteristic of the pre-modern world.

The risk environment of traditional cultures was dominated by the hazards of the physical world. Hobbes's celebrated observation that, in a state of nature, human life would be "nasty, brutish, and short" is not inaccurate if it is read as a description of the real life circumstances of many individuals in pre-modern cultures. Rates of infant mortality as well as death of women in childbirth were by modern standards extremely high. For those who survived childhood, life expectancy was relatively low and many people suffered from chronic illnesses as well as being vulnerable to infectious diseases of different kinds. There is some evidence that hunters and gatherers, especially those inhabiting naturally bountiful areas, may have been less subject to infectious illness than individuals living in fixed local communities or urban areas in larger pre-modern societies,[62] but even they were certainly not free from the range of endemic illnesses which abounded in pre-modern times. All types of pre-modern social order were affected, often in drastic ways, by the vagaries of climate and had little protection against natural disasters such as floods, storms, excessive rainfall, or drought.

To the unstable nature of social life in relation to the physical world we have to add, as a further source of insecurity, the prevalence of human violence. The major contrasts to be drawn here are between the larger premodern social orders and the modern social universe. The level of violence within and between hunting and gathering cultures appears generally to have been quite low, and there were no specialised warriors. With the appearance of armed soldiery, the situation is quite different. Most agrarian states were based in a very direct way upon military power. Yet, as was mentioned earlier, in such states the monopoly of control of the means of violence on the part of the ruling authorities was always far from complete. Such states were never internally pacified by the standards of modern nation-states. Few groups in the population could feel safe for lengthy periods from violence or the threat of violence from invading armies, marauders, local warlords, brigands, robbers, or pirates. Modern urban milieux are often considered dangerous because of the risk of being attacked or mugged. But not only is this level of violence characteristically minor as compared with many pre-modern settings; such milieux are only relatively small pockets within wider territorial areas, in which security against physical violence is vastly greater than ever was possible in regions of comparable size in the traditional world.

Finally we have to draw special attention to the dual influence of religion. If religious beliefs and practices commonly provide a refuge from the tribulations of day-to-day life, they can also, as noted, be an intrinsic source of anxiety and mental apprehension. In part this is due to the fact that religion permeates many aspects of social activity—the threats and dangers of nature, for example, may be experienced through the codes and symbols of religion. Mainly, however, it is because religion normally occupies the very psychological site of potential existential anxiety. How far religion creates its own specific terrors at this site is no doubt widely variable. Probably those forms of religious belief and practice which Weber called "salvation religions" are most prone to infect daily life with existential fears, invoking as they do a tension between sin and the promise of salvation in an afterlife. With the development of modern social institutions, something of a balance between trust and risk, security and danger persists. But the main elements involved are quite different from those which predominated in the pre-modern era. In conditions of modernity, just as in all cultural settings, human activities remain situated and contextualised. But the impact of the three great dynamic forces of modernity—the separation of time and space, disembedding mechanisms, and institutional reflexivity—disengages some basic forms of trust relation from the attributes of local contexts.

None of the four main foci of trust and ontological security in pre-modern settings have a comparable importance in circumstances of modernity. Kinship relations, for the majority of the population, remain important, especially within the nuclear family, but they are no longer the carriers of intensively organised social ties across time-space. Such a statement is indisputably valid, in spite of the caution with which the thesis that modernity produces the decline of the family has to be viewed and in spite of the fact that some local milieux continue to be the hub of substantial kinship networks of rights and obligations.

The primacy of place in pre-modern settings has been largely destroyed by disembedding and time-space distanciation. Place has become phantasmagoric because the structures by means of which it is constituted are no longer locally organised. The local and the global, in other words, have become inextricably intertwined. Feelings of close attachment to or identification with places still persist. But these are themselves disembedded: they do not just express locally based practices and involvements but are shot through with much more distant influences. Even the smallest of neighbourhood stores, for example, probably obtains its goods from all over the world. The local community is not a saturated environment of familiar, taken-for-granted meanings, but in some large part a locally-situated expression of distanciated relations. And everyone living in the different locales of modern societies is aware of this. Whatever security individuals experience as a result of the familiarity of place rests as much upon stable forms of disembedded relations as upon the particularities of location. If this is more obvious when one shops at the local supermarket than at the corner grocery, the difference is not a fundamental one.[63]

The declining impact of religion and tradition has been so frequently discussed in the literature of the social sciences that we can deal with this quite briefly. Secularisation is no doubt a complex matter and does not seem to result in the complete disappearance of religious thought and activity—probably because of the purchase of religion upon some of the existential questions previously referred to. Yet most of the situations of modern social life are manifestly incompatible with religion as a pervasive influence upon day-to-day life. Religious cosmology is supplanted by reflexively organised knowledge, governed by empirical observation and logical thought, and focused upon material technology and socially applied codes. Religion and tradition were always closely linked, and the latter is even more thoroughly undermined than the former by the reflexivity of modern social life, which stands in direct opposition to it.

The pre-modern "environment of risk" similarly becomes transformed. In conditions of modernity, the dangers we face no longer derive primarily from the world of nature. Of course, hurricanes, earthquakes, and other natural disasters still occur. But for the most part our relations with the physical world are radically different from those of previous ages—especially in the industrialised sectors of the globe, but in some degree everywhere. At first glance, the ecological dangers that we confront today might seem similar to the hazards of nature encountered in the pre-modern era. The contrast, however, is a very marked one. Ecological threats are the outcome of socially organised knowledge, mediated by the impact of industrialism upon the material environment. They are part of what I shall call a new *risk profile* introduced by the advent of modernity. By a risk profile I mean the particular portmanteau of threats or dangers characteristic of modern social life.

The threat of military violence remains part of the risk profile of modernity. However, its character has changed substantially, in conjunction with the altered nature of control of the means of violence in relation to war. We live today in a global military order in which, as a result of the industrialisation of war, the scale of the destructive power of the weaponry now diffused across the world is massively greater than has ever existed before. The possibility of nuclear conflict poses dangers no previous generations have had to face. Yet this development has coincided with processes of internal pacification within states. Civil war has become a relatively uncommon, if by no means unknown, phenomenon in developed nations; but in pre-modern times, at least after the first development of state organisations, something akin to civil war—divisions of military power, accompanied by frequent outbreaks of conflict—was more like the norm than the exception.

Risk and danger, as experienced in relation to ontological security, have become secularised along with most other aspects of social life. A world structured mainly by humanly created risks has little place for divine influences, or indeed for the magical propitiation of cosmic forces or spirits. It is central to modernity that risks can in principle be assessed in terms of generalisable knowledge about potential dangers—an outlook in which notions of *fortuna* mostly survive as marginal forms of superstition. Where risk is *known* to be risk, it is experienced differently from circumstances in which notions of *fortuna* prevail. To recognise the existence of a risk or set of risks is to accept not just the possibility that things might go wrong, but that this possibility cannot be eliminated. The phenomenology of such a situation is part of the cultural experience of modernity in general, discussed in more detail below. Even where the hold of traditional religion becomes relaxed, however, conceptions of fate do not wholly disappear. Precisely where risks are greatest—either in terms of the perceived probability that an unwelcome happening will occur or in terms of the devastating consequences that ensue if a given event goes awry—*fortuna* tends to return.

IV

*Abstract Systems and
the Transformation of Intimacy*

Abstract systems have provided a great deal of security in day-to-day life which was absent in pre-modern orders. A person can board a plane in London and reach Los Angeles some ten hours later and be fairly certain that not only will the journey be made safely, but that the plane will arrive quite close to a predetermined time. The passenger may perhaps only have a vague idea of where Los Angeles is, in terms of a global map. Only minimal preparations need to be made for the journey (obtaining passport, visa, air-ticket, and money)—no knowledge of the actual trajectory is necessary. A large amount of "surrounding" knowledge is required to be able to get on the plane, and this is knowledge which has been filtered back from expert systems to lay discourse and action. One has to know what an airport is, what an air-ticket is, and very many other things besides. But security on the journey itself does not depend upon mastery of the technical paraphernalia which make it possible.

Compare this with the task of an adventurer who undertook the same journey no more than three or four centuries ago. Although he would be the "expert," he might have little idea of where he was traveling *to*—and the very notion of "traveling" sounds oddly inapplicable. The journey would be fraught with dangers, and the risk of disaster or death very considerable. No one could participate in such an expedition who was not physically tough, resilient, and possessed of skills relevant to the conduct of the voyage.

Every time someone gets cash out of the bank or makes a deposit, casually turns on a light or a tap, sends a letter or makes a call on the telephone, she or he implicitly recognises the large areas of secure, coordinated actions and events that make modern social life possible. Of course, all sorts of hitches and breakdowns can also happen, and attitudes of scepticism or antagonism develop which produce the disengagement of individuals from one or more of these systems. But most of the time the taken-for-granted way in which everyday actions are geared into abstract systems bears witness to the effectiveness with which they operate (within the contexts of what is expected from them, because they also produce many kinds of unintended consequences).

Trust in abstract systems is the condition of time-space distanciation and of the large areas of security in day-to-day life which modern institutions offer as compared to the traditional world. The routines which are integrated with abstract systems are central to ontological security in conditions of modernity. Yet this situation also creates novel forms of psychological vulnerability, and trust in abstract systems is not psychologically rewarding in the way in which trust in persons is. I shall concentrate on the second of these points here, returning to the first later. To begin, I want to advance the following theorems: that there is a direct (although dialectical) connection between the globalising tendencies of modernity and what I shall call the *transformation of intimacy* in contexts of day-to-day life; that the transformation of intimacy can be analysed in terms of the building of trust mechanisms; and that personal trust relations, in such circumstances, are closely bound up with a situation in which the construction of the self becomes a reflexive project.

Trust and Personal Relations

In the early development of the human individual, basic trust in stable circumstances of self-identity and the surrounding environment—ontological security—does not in the first instance rest upon a sense of the continuity of things or events. Rather, as we have noted, it derives from personal trust and establishes a need for trust in others which no doubt endures, in some form or another, throughout life. Trust in persons, as Erikson emphasises, is built upon mutuality of response and involvement: faith in the integrity of another is a prime source of a feeling of integrity and authenticity of the self. Trust in abstract systems provides for the security of day-to-day reliability, but by its very nature cannot supply either the mutuality or intimacy which personal trust relations offer. In this respect traditional religions are plainly different from modern abstract systems, because their personalised figures allow for a direct transfer of individual trust, with large elements of mutuality. In the case of abstract systems, by contrast, trust presumes faith in impersonal principles, which "answer back" only in a statistical way when they do not deliver the outcomes which the individual seeks. This is one of the main reasons why individuals at access points normally go to great pains to show themselves to be trustworthy: they provide the link between personal and system trust.

Established sociological accounts of what I am terming the transformation of intimacy have mostly juxtaposed the communal character of traditional orders with the impersonality of modern social life. In capturing this conceptual distinction, Ferdinand Tönnies's contrast of *Gemeinschaft* and *Gesellschaft* is the classic source; whether they have used this specific terminology or not, others have drawn a very similar opposition. We may distinguish three main ways in which the contrast has been further fleshed out, each roughly linked to different political positions. One view, broadly associated with political conservatism, portrays the development of modernity as breaking down the old forms of "community," to the detriment of personal relations within modern societies. This standpoint was prominent in the late nineteenth century and still claims its representatives today. Thus Peter Berger, borrowing a notion from Arnold Gehlen, argues that the private sphere has become "deinstitutionalised," as a result of the dominance of large-scale bureaucratic organisations and the general influence of "mass society." The sphere of public life, on the other hand, has become "overly institutionalised." The result is that personal life becomes attenuated and bereft of firm reference points: there is a turning inward toward human subjectivity, and meaning and stability are sought in the inner self.[64]

Somewhat similar ideas have been advanced by authors standing on the other side of the political spectrum, sometimes influenced directly by Marxism. While their language is less that of "mass society" and more that of capitalism and commodification, their general thesis is not altogether different from that of the first group of writers. Modern institutions are seen to have taken over large areas of social life and drained them of the meaningful content they once had. The private sphere is thus left weakened and amorphous, even though many of life's prime satisfactions are to be found there because the world of "instrumental reason" is intrinsically limited in terms of the values it can realise. Jürgen Habermas's analysis of the separation of technical systems from the life-world is one variant of this position,[65] as is the view set out by Max Horkheimer a generation before. Speaking of friendship and intimacy, Horkheimer argues that in organised capitalism "personal initiative plays an ever smaller role in comparison to the plans of those in authority"; personal engagement with others "remains at best a hobby, a leisure-time trifle."[66]

The idea of the decline of community has been effectively criticised in the light of empirical research into city neighbourhoods, and many have drawn upon such investigations in order to challenge these two positions. Thus in criticising Louis Wirth's interpretation of the anonymous nature of urban life, Claude Fischer has sought to show that modern cities provide the means of generating new forms of communal life, largely unavailable in premodern settings.[67] According to the proponents of this third view, communal life either manages to survive under modern circumstances or actively becomes resurgent.

One of the chief difficulties with this debate concerns the terms in which it has been conducted. The "communal" has been contrasted with the "societal," the "impersonal" with the "personal"—and, from a somewhat different perspective, the "state" with "civil society"—as if these were all variants of the same thing. But the notion of community, as applied either to pre-modern or to modern cultures, comprises several sets of elements that must be distinguished. These are communal relations per se (which I have treated primarily in relation to place); kinship ties; relations of personal intimacy between peers (friendship); and relations of sexual intimacy. If we disentangle these, we can develop a standpoint different from any of those referred to above.

In the sense of an embedded affinity to place, "community" has indeed largely been destroyed, although one could quarrel about how far this process has gone in specific contexts. As Robert Sack observes,

To be an agent, one must be somewhere. This basic and integrative sense of place has come to be fragmented into complex, contradictory and disorienting parts. Space is becoming far more integrated and yet territorially fragmented. Places are specific or unique, yet in many senses they appear generic and alike. Places seem to be "out there", and yet they are humanly constructed. . . . Our society stores information about places, and yet we have little sense of place. And the landscapes that result from modern processes appear to be pastiches, disorienting, inauthentic and juxtaposed.[68]

A parallel conclusion must be reached about kinship, for reasons already adduced. The demonstration that kin ties of certain kinds remain strong in some contexts in modern societies hardly means that kinship plays the role it once did in structuring day-to-day life for the majority.

But how have these changes affected relations of personal and sexual intimacy? For these are not just simple extensions of community organisation or kinship. Friendship has rarely been studied by sociologists, but it provides an important clue to broad-ranging factors influencing personal life.[69] We have to understand the character of friendship in pre-modern contexts precisely in association with the local community and kinship. Trust in friends (the opposing term in such contexts being "enemies") was often of central importance. In traditional cultures, with the partial exception of some larger city neighbourhoods in agrarian states, there was a quite clear divide between insiders and outsiders or strangers. The wide arenas of nonhostile interaction with anonymous others characteristic of modern social activity did not exist. In these circumstances, friendship was often institutionalized and was seen as a means of creating more or less durable alliances with others against potentially hostile groups outside.

Institutionalised friendships were essentially forms of comradeship, such as blood brotherhoods or companions at arms. Whether institutionalised or not, friendship was characteristically based upon values of sincerity and honour. No doubt companionships sustained through emotional warmth and purely personal loyalty have existed in all cultures. But in the pre-modern world friendships were always liable to be placed in the service of risky endeavours where community or kinship ties were insufficient to provide the necessary resources—in forging economic connections, avenging wrongdoings, engaging in wars, and in many other activities. Sincerity is obviously likely to be a highly prized virtue in circumstances where the dividing lines between friend and enemy were generally distinct and tensionful. Codes of honour were in effect public guarantees of sincerity, even where the "goods" the friendship relation was called upon to deliver placed it under great strain.

The vast extension of abstract systems (including commodified markets) associated with modernity transforms the nature of friendship. Friendship is often a mode of reembedding, but is not directly involved in abstract systems themselves, which explicitly overcome dependency upon personal ties. The opposite of "friend" is no longer "enemy," nor even "stranger"; rather, it is "acquaintance," "colleague," or "someone I don't know." In accompaniment with this transition, honour is replaced by loyalty which has no other support save personal affection, and sincerity is replaced by what we can call *authenticity*: the requirement that the other be open and well-meaning. A friend is not someone who always speaks the truth, but someone who protects the emotional well-being of the other. The "good friend"—someone whose charity is forthcoming even in difficult times— is today's substitute for the "honourable companion."

We can relate this analysis back in a direct way to the discussion of trust. In pre-modern settings, basic trust is slotted into personalised trust relations in the community, kinship ties, and friendships. Although any of these social connections can involve emotional intimacy, this is not a condition of the maintaining of personal trust. Institutionalised personal ties and informal or informalised codes of sincerity and honour provide (potential, by no means always actual) frameworks of trust. Conversely, trust in others on a personal level is a prime means whereby social relations of a distanced sort, which stretch into "enemy territories," are established.

Trust and Personal Identity

With the development of abstract systems, trust in impersonal principles, as well as in anonymous others, becomes indispensable to social existence. Nonpersonalised trust of this sort is discrepant from basic trust. There is a strong psychological need to find others to trust, but institutionally organised personal connections are lacking, relative to pre-modern social situations. The point here is *not* primarily that many social characteristics which were previously part of everyday life or the "lifeworld" become drawn off and incorporated into abstract systems. Rather, the tissue and form of day-to-day life become reshaped in conjunction with wider social changes. Routines which are structured by abstract systems have an empty, unmoralised character—this much is valid in the idea that the impersonal increasingly swamps the personal. But this is not simply a diminishment of personal life in favour of impersonally organised systems—it is a genuine transformation of the nature of the personal itself. Personal relations whose main objective is sociability, informed by loyalty and authenticity, become as much a part of the social situations of modernity as the encompassing institutions of time-space distanciation.

It is quite wrong, however, to set off the impersonality of abstract systems against the intimacies of personal life as most existing sociological accounts tend to do. Personal life and the social ties it involves are deeply intertwined with the most far-reaching of abstract systems. It has long been the case, for example, that Western diets reflect global economic interchanges: "every cup of coffee contains within it the whole history of Western imperialism." With the accelerating globalisation of the past fifty years or so, the connections between personal life of the most intimate kind and disembedding mechanisms have intensified. As Ulrich Beck has observed, "The most intimate—say, nursing a child—and the most distant, most general—say a reactor accident in the Ukraine, energy politics—are now suddenly *directly* connected."[70]

What does this mean in terms of personal trust? The answer to this question is fundamental to the transformation of intimacy in the twentieth century. Trust in persons is not focused by personalised connections within the local community and kinship networks. Trust on a personal level becomes a project, to be "worked at" by the parties involved, and demands the *opening out of the individual to the other.* Where it cannot be controlled by fixed normative codes, trust has to be *won,* and the means of doing this is demonstrable warmth and openness. Our peculiar concern with "relationships," in the sense which that word has now taken on, is expressive of this phenomenon. Relationships are ties based upon trust, where trust is not pre-given but worked upon, and where the work involved means *a mutual process of self-disclosure.*

Given the strength of the emotions associated with sexuality, it is scarcely surprising that erotic involvements become a focal point for such self-disclosure. The transition to modern forms of erotic relations is generally thought to be associated with the formation of an ethos of romantic love, or with what Lawrence Stone calls "affective individualism." The ideal of romantic love is aptly described by Stone in the following way:

the notion that there is only one person in the world with whom one can unite at all levels; the personality of that person is so idealised that the normal faults and follies of human nature disappear from view; love is like a thunderbolt and strikes at first sight; love is the most important thing in the world, to which all other considerations, particularly material ones, should be sacrificed; and lastly, the giving of full rein to personal emotions is admirable, no matter how exaggerated and absurd the resulting conduct might appear to others.[71]

Characterised in this way, romantic love incorporates a cluster of values scarcely ever realisable in their totality. Rather than being an ethos associated in a continuous way with the rise of modern institutions, it seems essentially to have been a transitional phenomenon, bound up with a relatively early phase in the dissolution of the older forms of arranged marriage. Aspects of the "romantic love complex" as described by Stone have proved quite durable, but these have become increasingly meshed with the dynamics of personal trust described above. Erotic relations involve a progressive path of mutual discovery, in which a process of self-realisation on the part of the lover is as much a part of the experience as increasing intimacy with the loved one. Personal trust, therefore, has to be established through the process of self-enquiry: the discovery of oneself becomes a project directly involved with the reflexivity of modernity.

Interpretations of the quest for self-identity tend to divide in much the same way as views of the decline of community, to which they are often linked. Some see a preoccupation with self-development as an offshoot of the fact that the old communal orders have broken down, producing a narcissistic, hedonistic concern with the ego. Others reach much the same conclusion, but trace this end result to forms of social manipulation. Exclusion of the majority from the arenas where the most consequential policies are forged and decisions taken forces a concentration upon the self; this is a result of the powerlessness most people feel. In the words of Christopher Lasch:

> As the world takes on a more and more menacing appearance, life becomes a never-ending search for health and well-being through exercise, dieting, drugs, spiritual regimens of various kinds, psychic self-help, and psychiatry. For those who have withdrawn interest from the outside world except in so far as it remains a source of gratification and frustration, the state of their own health becomes an all-absorbing concern.[72]

Is the search for self-identity a form of somewhat pathetic narcissism, or is it, in some part at least, a subversive force in respect of modern institutions? Most of the debate about the issue has concentrated upon this question, and I shall return to it toward the end of this study. But for the moment we should see that there is something awry in Lasch's statement. A "search for health and well-being" hardly sounds compatible with a "withdrawal of interest in the outside world." The benefits of exercise or dieting are not personal discoveries but came from the lay reception of expert knowledge, as does the appeal of therapy or psychiatry. The spiritual regimens in question may be an eclectic assemblage, but include religions and cults from around the world. The outside world not only enters in here; it is an outside world vastly more extensive in character than anyone would have had contact with in the pre-modern era.

To summarise all this, the transformation of intimacy involves the following:

1. An intrinsic relation between the *globalising tendencies* of modernity and *localised events* in day-to-day life—a complicated, dialectical connection between the "extensional" and the "intensional."

2. The construction of the self as a *reflexive project*, an elemental part of the reflexivity of modernity; an individual must find her or his identity amid the strategies and options provided by abstract systems.

3. A drive towards self-actualisation, founded upon *basic trust*, which in personalised contexts can only be established by an "opening out" of the self to the other.

4. The formation of personal and erotic ties as "relationships," guided by the *mutuality of self-disclosure*.

5. *A concern for self-fulfilment*, which is not just a narcissistic defence against an externally threatening world, over which individuals have little control, but also in part a *positive appropriation* of circumstances in which globalised influences impinge upon everyday life.

Risk and Danger in the Modern World

How should we seek to analyse the "menacing appearance" of the contemporary world of which Lasch speaks? To do so means looking in more detail at the specific risk profile of modernity, which may be outlined in the following way:

1. *Globalisation of risk* in the sense of *intensity*: for example, nuclear war can threaten the survival of humanity.

2. *Globalisation of risk* in the sense of the *expanding number of contingent events* which affect everyone or at least large numbers of people on the planet: for example, changes in the global division of labour.

3. Risk stemming from the *created environment*, or *socialised nature*: the infusion of human knowledge into the material environment.

4. The development of *institutionalised risk environ-*

ments affecting the life-chances of millions: for example, investment markets.

5. *Awareness of risk* as *risk*: the "knowledge gaps" in risks cannot be converted into "certainties" by religious or magical knowledge.

6. The *well-distributed awareness of risk*: many of the dangers we face collectively are known to wide publics.

7. *Awareness of the limitations of expertise*: no expert system can be wholly expert in terms of the consequences of the adoption of expert principles.

If the disembedding mechanisms have provided large areas of security in the present-day world, the new array of risks which have thereby been brought into being are truly formidable. The main forms I have listed can be separated out into those that alter the objective distribution of risks (the first four items listed) and those that alter the experience of risk or the perception of perceived risks (the remaining three items).

What I have termed the intensity of risk is surely the basic element in the "menacing appearance" of the circumstances in which we live today. The possibility of nuclear war, ecological calamity, uncontainable population explosion, the collapse of global economic exchange, and other potential global catastrophes provide an unnerving horizon of dangers for everyone. As Beck has commented, globalised risks of this sort do not respect divisions between rich and poor or between regions of the world. The fact that "Chernobyl is everywhere" spells what he calls "the end of 'others' "—boundaries between those who are privileged and those who are not. The global intensity of certain kinds of risk transcends all social and economic differentials.[73] (Of course, this should not blind us to the fact that, in conditions of modernity, as in the pre-modern world, many risks are differentially distributed between the privileged and the underprivileged. Differential risk—in relation, for example, to levels of nutrition and susceptibility to illness—is a large part of what is actually meant by "privilege" and "underprivilege.")

Nuclear war is plainly the most potentially immediate and catastrophic of all current global dangers. Since the early 1980's it has been recognised that the climatic and environmental effects of a quite limited nuclear engagement could be very far-reaching. The detonation of a small number of warheads might produce irreversible environmental damage which could threaten the life of all complex animal species. The threshold for the occurrence of a "nuclear winter" has been calculated at between 500 and 2,000 warheads—less than 10 percent of the total held by the nuclear nations. It is even below the number possessed during the 1950's.[74] This circumstance wholly justifies the assertion that in such a context, there are no longer "others": the combatants and those uninvolved would all suffer.

The second category of globalised risks concerns the world-wide extension of risk environments, rather than the intensification of risk. All disembedding mechanisms take things out of the hands of any specific individuals or groups; and the more such mechanisms are of global scope, the more this tends to be so. Despite the high levels of security which globalised mechanisms can provide, the other side of the coin is that novel risks come into being: resources or services are no longer under local control and therefore cannot be locally refocused to meet unexpected contingencies, and there is a risk that the mechanism as a whole can falter, thus affecting everyone who characteristically makes use of it. Thus someone who has oil-fired central heating and no fireplaces is particularly vulnerable to changes in the price of oil. In circumstances such as the "oil crisis" of 1973, produced as a result of the actions of the OPEC cartel, all consumers of petroleum products are affected.

The first two categories in the risk profile concern the scope of risk environments; the next two are to do with changes in the type of risk environment. The category of the created environment, or "socialised nature"[75] refers to the altered character of the relation between human beings and the physical environment. The variety of ecological dangers in such a category derive from the transformation of nature by human knowledge systems. The sheer number of serious risks in respect of socialised nature is quite daunting: radiation from major accidents at nuclear power-stations or from nuclear waste; chemical pollution of the seas sufficient to destroy the phytoplankton that renews much of the oxygen in the atmosphere; a "greenhouse effect" deriving from atmospheric pollutants which attack the ozone layer, melting part of the ice caps and flooding vast areas; the destruction of large areas of rain forest which are a basic source of renewable oxygen; and the exhaustion of millions of acres of topsoil as a result of widespread use of artificial fertilisers.

Other significant hazards could be mentioned. In passing, we should note two things about this list and about the risk of nuclear war. One is the numbing feeling, almost one of boredom, which such a list is likely to induce in the reader—a phenomenon which relates to the sixth point in the risk profile, the fact that awareness of many generalised kinds of risk is now widespread among the population at large. Even the noting of this numbness has become something of a commonplace: "Listing the dangers we face has itself a deadening effect. It becomes a litany which is only half listened to because it seems so familiar. We are bombarded constantly with these problems so that they become, in their intractability, part of the background."[76] The second point is that virtually all the risks mentioned, including the risk of a nuclear war as such, are controversial in terms of any assessment that might be made of strict probabilities. We can never be sure that deterrence "works," short of the actual occurrence of a nuclear combat—which shows that it does not; the hypothesis of a nuclear winter will remain just that unless its actual occurrence makes any such consideration altogether irrelevant. I shall revert to these observations subsequently, since both are important in relation to the experience and perception of risk.

Within the various spheres of modern institutions, risks do not just exist as hazards resulting from the imperfect operation of disembedding mechanisms, but also as "closed," institutionalised arenas of action. In such spheres, as was mentioned previously, risks are actually created by normatively sanctioned forms of activity—as in the case of gambling or sports. Investment markets represent easily the most prominent example in modern social life. All business firms, save for some types of nationalised industry, and all investors, operate in an environment in which each has to outguess others in order to maximise economic returns. The uncertainties involved in investment decisions derive in some part from difficulties in anticipating extraneous events, such as technological innovations, but are also part of the nature of markets themselves. As an approach to social analysis, game theory probably works best when applied to such situations, in which agents are trying to outguess others, knowing that at the same time these others are endeavouring to outguess them.

However, there are various other circumstances in which this situation applies—in some aspects of voting procedures, for example, and most notably in the arms race between the two superpowers. If one excludes the actual risk of war itself, which from this point of view is extraneous, the arms race is based upon mutual outguessing, each party basing its strategies upon its assessment of the likely strategies of the other. Like the arms race, the institutionalised risk environment of markets cannot be kept confined to its own "proper sphere." Not only do extraneous risks force themselves in, but the outcomes of decisions within the institutionalised framework constantly affect those outside. Although I shall not discuss this in the present context, it matters a great deal for the economic prosperity of many millions of people how far the coordination of investment decisions represents a form of collective rationality and how far investment markets are mere lotteries, governed by Keynes's "animal spirits."

In terms of the experience of risk, far more could be said than I have the opportunity to analyse here. The three aspects of the awareness of risk indicated in the risk profile above, however, are immediately relevant to the arguments developed in this study thus far and to subsequent sections. The fact that risks—including in this regard many different forms of activity—are generally accepted by the lay population to be risks is a major aspect of the disjuncture between the pre-modern and the modern worlds. High-risk enterprises undertaken in traditional cultures may sometimes have occurred in a secular domain, but more typically were carried out under the auspices of religion or magic. How far individuals may have been prepared to vest trust in particular religious or magical prescriptions in specific risk domains was no doubt widely variable. But religion and magic very often provided a way of sealing over the uncertainties entailed in risky endeavours, thus translating the experience of risk into feelings of relative security. Where risk is known *as* risk, this mode of generating confidence in hazardous actions is by definition unavailable. In a predominantly secular milieu, there are various ways of trying to transmute risk into providential *fortuna*, but they remain half-hearted superstitions rather than truly effective psychological supports. People in occupations entailing life-threatening risks, such as steeplejacks, or in enterprises where the outcome is structurally indeterminate, like sports players, quite often have recourse to charms or superstitious rituals, to "influence" the outcomes of what they do. But they might very well be scorned by others if they make these practices too public.

We can take the final two points in the risk profile together. Widespread lay knowledge of modern risk environments leads to awareness of the limits of expertise and forms one of the "public relations" problems that has to be faced by those who seek to sustain lay trust in expert systems. The faith that supports trust in expert systems involves a blocking off of the ignorance of the lay person when faced with the claims of expertise; but realisation of the areas of ignorance which confront the experts themselves, as individual practitioners and in terms of overall fields of knowledge, may weaken or undermine that faith on the part of lay individuals. Experts often take risks "on behalf" of lay clients while concealing, or fudging over, the true nature of those risks or even the fact that there are risks at all. More damaging than the lay discovery of this kind of concealment is the circumstance where the full extent of a particular set of dangers and the risks associated with them is not realised by the experts. For in this case what is in question is not only the limits of, or the gaps in, expert knowledge, but an inadequacy which compromises the very idea of expertise.[77]

Risk and Ontological Security

In what ways does this array of risks impinge upon lay trust in expert systems and feelings of ontological security? The baseline for analysis has to be the *inevitability* of living with dangers which are *remote* from the control not only of individuals, but also of large organisations, including states; and which are *of high intensity* and *life-threatening* for millions of human beings and potentially for the whole of humanity. The facts that these are not risks anyone *chooses* to run and that there are, in Beck's terms, no "others" who could be held responsible, attacked, or blamed reinforce the sense of foreboding which so many have noted as a characteristic of the current age.[78] Nor is it surprising that some of those who hold to religious beliefs are inclined to see the potential for global disaster as an expression of the wrath of God. For the high consequence global risks which we all now run are key elements of the runaway, juggernaut character of modernity, and no specific individuals or groups are responsible for them or can be constrained to "set things right."

How can we constantly keep in the forefront of our

minds dangers which are enormously threatening, yet so remote from individual control? The answer is that most of us cannot. People who worry all day, every day, about the possibility of nuclear war, as was noted earlier, are liable to be thought disturbed. While it would be difficult to deem irrational someone who was constantly and consciously anxious in this way, this outlook would paralyse ordinary day-to-day life. Even a person who raises the topic at a social gathering is prone to be thought hysterical or gauche. In Carolyn See's novel *Golden Days*, which finishes in the aftermath of a nuclear war, the main character relates her fear of a nuclear holocaust to another guest at a dinner party:

Her eyes were wide. She gazed at me with terrific concentration. "Yes", she said, "I understand what you're saying. I get it. But isn't it true that your fear of nuclear war is a metaphor for all the *other* fears that plague us today?"
My mind has never been exactly fine. But sometimes it has been good. "No", I said. I may have shouted it through the beautiful, sheltered room. "It's my view that the other fears, all those of which we have spoken, are a metaphor of my fear of nuclear war!"
She stared at me incredulously, but was spared the difficulty of a response when we were all called to a very pleasant late supper.[79]

The incredulity of the dinner party guest has nothing to do with the argument expressed; it registers disbelief that anyone should become emotional about such an issue in such a setting.

The large majority of people do not spend much of their time, on a conscious level at least, worrying about nuclear war or about the other major hazards for which it may or may not be a metaphor. The need to get on with the more local practicalities of day-to-day life is no doubt one reason, but much more is involved psychologically. In a secular environment, low-probability high-consequence risks tend to conjure up anew a sense of *fortuna* closer to the pre-modern outlook than that cultivated by minor superstitions. A sense of "fate," whether positively or negatively tinged—a vague and generalised sense of trust in distant events over which one has no control—relieves the individual of the burden of engagement with an existential situation which might otherwise be chronically disturbing. Fate, a feeling that things will take their own course anyway, thus reappears at the core of a world which is supposedly taking rational control of its own affairs. Moreover, this surely exacts a price on the level of the unconscious, since it essentially presumes the repression of anxiety. The sense of dread which is the antithesis of basic trust is likely to infuse unconscious sentiments about the uncertainties faced by humanity as a whole.[80]

Low-probability high-consequence risks will not disappear in the modern world, although in an optimal scenario they could be minimised. Thus, were it to be the case that all existing nuclear weapons were done away with, no other weapons of comparable destructive force were invented, and no comparably catastrophic disturbances of socialised nature were to loom, a profile of global danger would still exist. For if it is accepted that the eradication of established technical knowledge could not be achieved, nuclear weaponry could be reconstructed at any point. Moreover, any major technological initiative could thoroughly disturb the overall orientation of global affairs. The juggernaut effect is inherent in modernity, for reasons I shall amplify in the next section of this work.

The heavily counterfactual character of the most consequential risks is closely bound up with the numbness that a listing of them tends to promote. In mediaeval times, the invention of hell and damnation as the fate of the unbeliever in the afterlife was "real." Yet things are different with the most catastrophic dangers which face us today. The greater the danger, measured not in terms of probability of occurrence but in terms of its generalised threat to human life, the more thoroughly counterfactual it is. The risks involved are necessarily "unreal," because we could only have clear demonstration of them if events occurred that are too terrible to contemplate. Relatively small-scale events, such as the dropping of atomic bombs on Hiroshima and Nagasaki or the accidents at Three Mile Island or Chernobyl, give us some sense of what could happen. But these do not in any way bear upon the necessarily counterfactual character of other, more cataclysmic happenings—the main basis of their "unreality" and the narcotising effects produced by the repeated listing of risks. As Susan Sontag remarks, "A permanent modern scenario: apocalypse looms —and it doesn't occur. And still it looms. . . . Apocalypse is now a long-running serial: not 'Apocalypse Now', but 'Apocalypse from now on' ".[81]

Adaptive Reactions

It is not clear that there are significant differences between lay individuals and experts regarding the range of adaptive reactions to the risk profile of modernity. For reasons just stated, the most worrying counterfactuals cannot be translated into situations of empirical testing, and those expert in the particular fields in question are often likely to be as divided about them as are less-informed individuals. The possible adaptive reactions seem to be fourfold.

The first might be called *pragmatic acceptance* and is the outlook described by Lasch. It involves a concentration, as he puts it, on "surviving." What is at issue here is not so much a withdrawal from the outside world as a pragmatic participation which maintains a focus on day-to-day problems and tasks. Raymond Williams speaks of such an orientation as "Plan X," "a new politics of strategic advantage"—the belief that much that goes on in the modern world is outside anyone's control, so that temporary gains are all that can be planned or hoped for. In his view this applies not only to the attitudes of many lay persons, but to major domains of strategic action, such as the arms race itself.[82]

Pragmatic acceptance is not without psychological costs, for reasons already mentioned. It implies a numbness frequently reflecting deep underlying anxieties, which in some individuals repeatedly surface at a conscious level. In Dorothy Rowe's study of how awareness of the possibility of nuclear war affects everyday life, a typical reaction is this: "The only honest answer I can give you as to how I can manage to live with the possibility of it is that I don't think about it, because to do so is frightening. This doesn't work all the time, of course, and frequently I have appalling visions of what it would be like if these weapons were used."[83] Pragmatic acceptance is compatible with either an underlying feeling-tone of pessimism or with the nourishment of hope—which may coexist with it ambivalently.

A second adaptive reaction can be termed *sustained optimism*, which is essentially the persistence of the attitudes of the Enlightenment, a continued faith in providential reason in spite of whatever dangers threaten at the current time. This is the outlook of those experts, for example, who hold that nuclear deterrence has worked thus far and will continue to work for the indefinite future; or those who have criticised "doomsday" ecological scenarios in favour of the view that social and technological solutions can be found for the major global problems.[84] For lay individuals, it is a perspective which continues to hold great resonance and emotional appeal, based as it is upon a conviction that unfettered rational thought and particularly science offer sources of long-term security that no other orientations can match. However, certain types of religious ideals also readily find an elective affinity with sustained optimism.

An opposite set of attitudes is that of *cynical pessimism*. Unlike pragmatic acceptance, this presumes a direct involvement with the anxieties provoked by high consequence dangers. Cynicism is not indifference. Nor is it necessarily doom-laden, although it is hardly compatible with blunt optimism. Cynicism is a mode of dampening the emotional impact of anxieties through either a humorous or a world-weary response to them. It lends itself to parody, as in the film *Dr. Strangelove* and in many forms of "black humour," but also to an anachronistic celebration of the delights of the here-and-now, cocking a snout at the future-oriented perspectives of modernity. In some of these guises, cynicism is detachable from pessimism and can coexist with a kind of desperate hopefulness. Pessimism is also in principle separable from cynicism, if defined as the conviction that, whatever one does, things will turn out badly.[85] Yet unlike the association of optimism and Enlightenment ideals, it is difficult to give a content to pessimism, apart from nostalgia for ways of life that are disappearing or a negative attitude toward what is to come. Pessimism is not a formula for action, and in an extreme form it leads only to paralysing depression. Conjoined to cynicism, however, it provides an outlook with practical implications. Cynicism takes the edge off pessimism, because of its emotionally neutralising nature and because of its potential for humour.

Finally, we can distinguish what I shall call *radical engagement*, by which I mean an attitude of practical contestation towards perceived sources of danger. Those taking a stance of radical engagement hold that, although we are beset by major problems, we can and should mobilise either to reduce their impact or to transcend them. This is an optimistic outlook, but one bound up with contestory action rather than a faith in rational analysis and discussion. Its prime vehicle is the social movement.

A Phenomenology of Modernity

Two images of what it feels like to live in the world of modernity have dominated the sociological literature, yet both of them seem less than adequate. One is that of Weber, according to which the bonds of rationality are drawn tighter and tighter, imprisoning us in a featureless cage of bureaucratic routine. Among the three major founders of modern sociology, Weber saw most clearly the significance of expertise in modern social development and used it to outline a phenomenology of modernity. Everyday experience, according to Weber, retains its colour and spontaneity, but only on the perimeter of the "steel-hard" cage of bureaucratic rationality. The image has a great deal of power and has, of course, featured strongly in fictional literature in the twentieth century as well as in more directly sociological discussions. There are many contexts of modern institutions which are marked by bureaucratic fixity. But they are far from all-pervasive, and even in the core settings of its application, namely, large-scale organisations, Weber's characterisation of bureaucracy is inadequate. Rather than tending inevitably towards rigidity, organisations produce areas of autonomy and spontaneity—which are actually often less easy to achieve in smaller groups. We owe this counterinsight to Durkheim, as well as to subsequent empirical study of organisations. The closed climate of opinion within some small groups and the modes of direct sanction available to its members fix the horizons of action much more narrowly and firmly than in larger organisational settings.

The second is the image of Marx—and of many others, whether they regard themselves as Marxist or not. According to this portrayal, modernity is seen as a monster. More limpidly perhaps than any of his contemporaries, Marx perceived how shattering the impact of modernity would be, and how irreversible. At the same time, modernity was for Marx what Habermas has aptly called an "unfinished project." The monster can be tamed, since what human beings have created they can always subject to their own control. Capitalism, simply, is an irrational way to run the modern world, because it substitutes the whims of the market for the controlled fulfilment of human need.

For these images I suggest we should substitute that of the juggernaut*—a runaway engine of enormous power which, collectively as human beings, we can drive to some extent but which also threatens to rush out of our control and which could rend itself asunder. The juggernaut crushes those who resist it, and while it sometimes seems to have a steady path, there are times when it veers away erratically in directions we cannot foresee. The ride is by no means wholly unpleasant or unrewarding; it can often be exhilarating and charged with hopeful anticipation. But, so long as the institutions of modernity endure, we shall never be able to control completely either the path or the pace of the journey. In turn, we shall never be able to feel entirely secure, because the terrain across which it runs is fraught with risks of high consequence. Feelings of ontological security and existential anxiety will coexist in ambivalence.

The juggernaut of modernity is not all of one piece, and here the imagery lapses, as does any talk of a single path which it runs. It is not an engine made up of integrated machinery, but one in which there is a tensionful, contradictory, push-and-pull of different influences. Any attempt to capture the experience of modernity must begin from this view, which derives ultimately from the dialectics of space and time, as expressed in the time-space constitution of modern institutions. I shall sketch a phenomenology of modernity in terms of four dialectically related frameworks of experience, each of which connects in an integral way with the preceding discussion in this study:

*The term comes from the Hindi *Jagannāth*, "lord of the world," and is a title of Krishna; an idol of this deity was taken each year through the streets on a huge car, which followers are said to have thrown themselves under, to be crushed beneath the wheels.

Displacement and reembedding: the intersection of estrangement and familiarity.

Intimacy and impersonality: the intersection of personal trust and impersonal ties.

Expertise and reappropriation: the intersection of abstract systems and day-to-day knowledgeability.

Privatism and engagement: the intersection of pragmatic acceptance and activism.

Modernity "dis-places" in the sense previously analysed—place becomes phantasmagoric. Yet this is a double-layered, or ambivalent, experience rather than simply a loss of community. We can see this clearly only if we keep in mind the contrasts between the pre-modern and the modern described earlier. What happens is not simply that localised influences drain away into the more impersonalised relations of abstract systems. Instead, the very tissue of spatial experience alters, conjoining proximity and distance in ways that have few close parallels in prior ages. There is a complex relation here between familiarity and estrangement. Many aspects of life in local contexts continue to have a familiarity and ease to them, grounded in the day-to-day routines individuals follow. But the sense of the familiar is one often mediated by time-space distanciation. It does not derive from the particularities of localised place. And this experience, so far as it seeps into general awareness, is simultaneously disturbing and rewarding. The reassurance of the familiar, so important to a sense of ontological security, is coupled with the realisation that what is comfortable and nearby is actually an expression of distant events and was "placed into" the local environment rather than forming an organic development within it. The local shopping mall is a milieu in which a sense of ease and security is cultivated by the layout of the buildings and the careful planning of public places. Yet everyone who shops there is aware that most of the shops are chain stores, which one might find in any city, and indeed that innumerable shopping malls of similar design exist elsewhere.

A feature of displacement is our insertion into globalised cultural and information settings, which means that familiarity and place are much less consistently connected than hitherto. This is less a phenomenon of estrangement from the local than one of integration within globalised "communities" of shared experience. The boundaries of concealment and disclosure become altered, since many erstwhile quite distinct activities are juxtaposed in unitary public domains. The newspaper and the sequence of television programmes over the day are the most obvious concrete examples of this phenomenon, but it is generic to the time-space organisation of modernity. We are all familiar with events, with actions, and with the visible appearance of physical settings thousands of miles away from where we happen to live. The coming of electronic media has undoubtedly accentuated these aspects of displacement, since they override presence so instantaneously and at such distance. As Joshua Meyrowitz points out, a person on the telephone to another, perhaps on the opposite side of the world, is more closely bound to that distant other than to another individual in the same room (who may be asking, "Who is it? What's she saying?" and so forth).

The counterpart of displacement is reembedding. The disembedding mechanisms lift social relations and the exchange of information out of specific time-space contexts, but at the same time provide new opportunities for their reinsertion. This is another reason why it is a mistake to see the modern world as one in which large, impersonal systems increasingly swallow up most of personal life. The self-same processes that lead to the destruction of older city neighbourhoods and their replacement by towering office-blocks and skyscrapers often permit the gentrification of other areas and a recreation of locality. Although the picture of tall, impersonal clusters of city-centre buildings is often presented as the epitome of the landscape of modernity, this is a mistake. Equally characteristic is the recreation of places of relative smallness and informality. The very means of transportation which help to dissolve the connection between locality and kinship provide the possibility for reembedding, by making it easy to visit "close" relatives who are far away.

Parallel comments can be made about the intersection of intimacy and impersonality in modern contexts of action. It is simply not true that in conditions of modernity we live increasingly in a "world of strangers." We are not required more and more to exchange intimacy for impersonality in the contacts with others we routinely make in the course of our day-to-day lives. Something much more complex and subtle is involved. Day-to-day contacts with others in pre-modern settings were normally based upon a familiarity stemming in part from the nature of place. Yet contacts with familiar others probably rarely facilitated the level of intimacy we associate with personal and sexual relations today. The "transformation of intimacy" of which I have spoken is contingent upon the very distancing which the disembedding mechanisms bring about, combined with the altered environments of trust which they presuppose. There are some very obvious ways in which intimacy and abstract systems interact. Money, for example, can be spent to purchase the expert services of a psychologist who guides the individual in an exploration of the inner universe of the intimate and the personal.

A person walks the streets of a city and encounters perhaps thousands of people in the course of a day, people she or he has never met before—"strangers" in the modern sense of that term. Or perhaps that individual strolls along less crowded thoroughfares, idly scrutinising passersby and the diversity of products for sale in the shops— Baudelaire's *flâneur*. Who could deny that these experiences are an integral element of modernity? Yet the world "out there"—the world that shades off into indefinite time-space from the familiarity of the home and the local neighbourhood—is not at all a purely impersonal one. On the contrary, intimate relationships can be sustained at distance (regular and sustained contact can be made with other individuals at virtually any point on the earth's surface—as well as some below and above), and personal ties are continually forged with others with whom one was previously unacquainted. We live in a *peopled* world, not merely one of anonymous, blank faces, and the interpolation of abstract systems into our activities is intrinsic to bringing this about.

In relations of intimacy of the modern type, trust is always ambivalent, and the possibility of severance is more or less ever present. Personal ties can be ruptured, and ties of intimacy returned to the sphere of impersonal contacts—in the broken love affair, the intimate suddenly becomes again a stranger. The demand of "opening oneself up" to the other which personal trust relations now presume, the injunction to hide nothing from the other, mix reassurance and deep anxiety. Personal trust demands a level of self-understanding and self-expression which must itself be a source of psychological tension. For mutual self-revelation is combined with the need for reciprocity and support; yet the two are frequently incompatible. Torment and frustration interweave themselves with the need for trust in the other as the provider of care and support.

Deskilling and Reskilling in Everyday Life

Expertise is part of intimacy in conditions of modernity, as is shown not just by the huge variety of forms of psychotherapy and counseling available, but by the plurality of books, articles, and television programmes providing technical information about "relationships." Does this mean that, as Habermas puts it, abstract systems "colonise" a pre-existing "life-world," subordinating personal decisions to technical expertise? It does not. The reasons are twofold. One is that modern institutions do not just implant themselves into a "life-world," the residues of which remain much the same as they always were. Changes in the nature of day-to-day life also affect the disembedding mechanisms, in a dialectical interplay. The second reason is that technical expertise is continuously reappropriated by lay agents as part of their routine dealings with abstract systems. No one can become an expert, in the sense of the possession either of full expert knowledge or of the appropriate formal credentials, in more than a few small sectors of the immensely complicated knowledge systems which now exist. Yet no one can interact with abstract systems without mastering some of the rudiments of the principles upon which they are based.

Sociologists often suppose that, in contrast to the pre-modern era, where many things were mysteries, today we live in a world from which mystery has retreated and where the way "the world works" can (in principle) be exhaustively known. But this is not true for either the lay person or the expert, if we consider their experience as individuals. To all of us living in the modern world things are specifically *opaque*, in a way that was not the case previously. In pre-modern environments the "local knowledge," to adapt a phrase from Clifford Geertz,[86] which individuals possessed was rich, varied, and adapted to the requirements of living in the local milieu. But how many of us today when we switch on the light know much about where the electricity supply comes from or even, in a technical sense, what electricity actually is?

Yet, although "local knowledge" cannot be of the same order as it once was, the sieving off of knowledge and skill from everyday life is not a one-way process. Nor are individuals in modern contexts less knowledgeable about their local milieux than their counterparts in pre-modern cultures. Modern social life is a complex affair, and there are many "filter-back" processes whereby technical knowledge, in one shape or another, is reappropriated by lay persons and routinely applied in the course of their day-to-day activities. As was mentioned earlier, the interaction between expertise and reappropriation is strongly influenced, among other things, by experiences at access points. Economic factors may decide whether a person learns to fix her or his car engine, rewire the electrical system of the house, or fix the roof; but so do the levels of trust that an individual vests in the particular expert systems and known experts involved. Processes of reappropriation relate to all aspects of social life—for example, medical treatment, child-rearing, or sexual pleasure.

For the ordinary individual, all this does not add up to feelings of secure control over day-to-day life circumstances. Modernity expands the arenas of personal fulfilment and of security in respect of large swathes of day-to-day life. But the lay person—and *all* of us are lay persons in respect of the vast majority of expert systems—must ride the juggernaut. The lack of control which many of us feel about some of the circumstances of our lives is real.

It is against this backdrop that we should understand patterns of privatism and engagement. A sense of "survival," in Lasch's use of this term, cannot be absent from our thoughts all of the time in a world in which, for the indefinite future, survival is a real and inescapable issue. On the level of the unconscious—even, and perhaps especially, among those whose attitude is one of pragmatic acceptance towards high-consequence risks—the relation to survival probably exists as existential dread. For basic trust in the continuity of the world must be anchored in the simple conviction that it will continue, and this is something of which we cannot be entirely sure. Saul Bellow remarks in the novel *Herzog*, "The revolution of nuclear terror returns the metaphysical dimension to us. All practical activity has reached this culmination: everything may go now, civilisation, history, nature. Now to recall Mr. Kierkegaard's question . . ."[87] "Mr. Kierkegaard's question" is, how do we avoid the dread of nonexistence, considered not just as individual death but as an existential void? The possibility of global calamity, whether by nuclear war or other means, prevents us from reassuring ourselves with the assumption that the life of the species inevitably surpasses that of the individual.

How remote that possibility is, literally no one knows. So long as there is deterrence, there must be the chance of war, because the notion of deterrence only makes sense if the parties involved are in principle prepared to use the weaponry they hold. Once again, no one, no matter how "expert" about the logistics of weapons and military organisation or about world politics, can say whether deterrence "works," because the most that can be said is that so far there has been no war. Awareness of these inherent uncertainties does not escape the lay population, however vague that awareness might be.

Balanced against the deep anxieties which such circumstances must produce in virtually everyone is the psychological prop of the feeling that "there's nothing that I as an individual can do," and that at any rate the risk must be very slight. Business-as-usual, as I have pointed out, is a prime element in the stabilising of trust and ontological security, and this no doubt applies in respect of high-consequence risks just as it does in other areas of trust relations.

Yet obviously even high-consequence risks are not only remote contingencies, which can be ignored in daily life, albeit at some probable psychological cost. Some such risks, and many others which are potentially life-threatening for individuals or otherwise significantly affect them, intrude right into the core of day-to-day activities. This is true, for example, of any pollution damage which affects the health of adults or children, and anything which produces toxic contents in food or affects its nutritional properties. It is also true of a multitude of technological changes that influence life chances, such as reproductive technologies. The mix of risk and opportunity is so complex in many of the circumstances involved that it is extremely difficult for individuals to know how far to vest trust in particular prescriptions or systems, and how far to suspend it. How can one manage to eat "healthily," for example, when all kinds of food are said to have toxic qualities of one sort or another and when what is held to be "good for you" by nutritional experts varies with the shifting state of scientific knowledge?

Trust and risk, opportunity and danger—these polar, paradoxical features of modernity permeate all aspects of day-to-day life, once more reflecting an extraordinary interpolation of the local and the global. Pragmatic acceptance can be sustained towards most of the abstract systems that impinge on individuals' lives, but by its very nature such an attitude cannot be carried on all the while and in respect of all areas of activity. For incoming expert information is often fragmentary or inconsistent,* as is the recycled knowledge which colleagues, friends, and intimates pass on to one another. On a personal level, decisions must be taken and policies forged. Privatism, the avoidance of contestatory engagement—which can be supported by attitudes of basic optimism, pessimism, or pragmatic acceptance—can serve the purposes of day-to-

---

*Consider, as one among an indefinite range of examples, the case of cyclamate, an artificial sweetener, and the U.S. authorities. Cyclamate was widely used in the United States until 1970, and the Food and Drug Administration classified it as "generally recognised as safe." The attitude of the FDA changed when scientific research concluded that rats given large doses of the substance were prone to certain types of cancer. Cyclamate was banned from use in foodstuffs. As more and more people began to drink low-calorie beverages in the 1970's and early 1980's, however, manufacturers exerted pressure on the FDA to change its stance. In 1984, a committee of the FDA decided that cyclamate was not after all a cancer-producing agent. A year later, the National Academy of Sciences intervened, reaching yet a different conclusion. In its report on the subject, the Academy declared that cyclamate is unsafe when used with saccharin, although probably harmless when used on its own as a sweetener. See James Bellini, *High Tech Holocaust* (London: Tarrant, 1986).

day "survival" in many respects. But it is likely to be interspersed with phases of active engagement, even on the part of those most prone to attitudes of indifference or cynicism. For, to repeat, in respect of the balance of security and danger which modernity introduces into our lives, there are no longer "others"—no one can be completely outside. Conditions of modernity, in many circumstances, provoke activism rather than privatism, because of modernity's inherent reflexivity and because there are many opportunities for collective organisation within the polyarchic systems of modern nation-states.

Objections to Post-Modernity

Let me at this point return briefly to issues raised near the beginning of the book and at the same time look ahead to the closing sections. I have sought to develop an interpretation of the current era which challenges the usual views of the emergence of post-modernity. As ordinarily understood, conceptions of post-modernity—which mostly have their origin in post-structuralist thought—involve a number of distinct strands. I compare this conception of post-modernity (PM) with my alternative position, which I shall call radicalised modernity (RM), in Table 2, which follows on p. 150.

TABLE 2
A Comparison of Conceptions of
"Post-Modernity" (PM) and "Radicalised Modernity" (RM)

PM	RM
1. Understands current transitions in epistemological terms or as dissolving epistemology altogether.	1. Identifies the institutional developments which create a sense of fragmentation and dispersal.
2. Focuses upon the centrifugal tendencies of current social transformations and their dislocating character.	2. Sees high modernity as a set of circumstances in which dispersal is dialectically connected to profound tendencies towards global integration.
3. Sees the self as dissolved or dismembered by the fragmenting of experience.	3. Sees the self as more than just a site of intersecting forces; active processes of reflexive self-identity are made possible by modernity.
4. Argues for the contextuality of truth claims or sees them as "historical."	4. Argues that the universal features of truth claims force themselves upon us in an irresistible way given the primacy of problems of a global kind. Systematic knowledge about these developments is not precluded by the reflexivity of modernity.
5. Theorises powerlessness which individuals feel in the face of globalising tendencies.	5. Analyses a dialectic of powerlessness and empowerment, in terms of both experience and action.
6. Sees the "emptying" of day-to-day life as a result of the intrusion of abstract systems.	6. Sees day-to-day life as an active complex of reactions to abstract systems, involving appropriation as well as loss.
7. Regards coordinated political engagement as precluded by the primacy of contextuality and dispersal.	7. Regards coordinated political engagement as both possible and necessary, on a global level as well as locally.
8. Defines post-modernity as the end of epistemology/the individual/ethics.	8. Defines post-modernity as possible transformations moving "beyond" the institutions of modernity.

V

Riding the Juggernaut

How far can we—where "we" means humanity as a whole—harness the juggernaut, or at least direct it in such a way as to minimise the dangers and maximise the opportunities which modernity offers to us? Why, in any case, do we currently live in such a runaway world, so different from that which the Enlightenment thinkers anticipated? Why has the generalising of "sweet reason" not produced a world subject to our prediction and control?

Several factors suggest themselves, none of which, however, have anything to do with the idea that we no longer have any viable methods of sustaining knowledge claims in the sense of Lyotard and others. The first might be termed *design faults*. Modernity is inseparable from the abstract systems that provide for the disembedding of social relations across space and time and span both socialised nature and the social universe. Perhaps too many of these suffer from design faults which, when they lead systems to go wrong, send us spinning away from our projected paths of development? Now plainly we can apply a notion of design faults to social as well as natural systems, where the former are established with definite "ends in view." Any organisation can in principle be assessed in terms of how far it effectively reaches certain goals or provides certain services. Any aspect of socialised nature can in principle be evaluated in terms of how far it meets particular human needs and produces no unwanted end results. In both contexts, design faults are undoubtedly very common. In the case of systems depending upon socialised nature, there seems no reason, again in principle, why design faults should not be eradicated. The situation in respect of social systems is more complicated and difficult, as we shall see.

A second factor is what we might call *operator failure*. Any abstract system, no matter how well designed it is, can fail to work as it is supposed to do because those who operate it make mistakes. This also applies both to social and natural systems. Unlike design faults, operator failure appears to be ineradicable. Good design can make the possibility of operator failure very low, and so can rigorous training and discipline; but so long as human beings are involved, the risk must be there. In the case of the Chernobyl incident, the root cause of the disaster was a mistake made in the operating of the emergency shutdown systems. Mathematical calculations of risk, such as the risks of human mortality attaching to competing methods of generating power, can be carried out about the working of physical systems. But the element of operator failure cannot effectively be incorporated into such calculations.

However, neither design faults nor operator failure are the most important elements producing the erratic character of modernity. The two most significant influences are those referred to briefly earlier: *unintended conse-*

quences and the *reflexivity* or *circularity of social knowl-edge*. Design faults and operator failure clearly fall within the category of unintended consequences, but the category includes much more. No matter how well a system is designed and no matter how efficient its operators, the consequences of its introduction and functioning, in the contexts of the operation of other systems and of human activity in general, cannot be wholly predicted. One reason for this is the complexity of systems and actions that make up world society. But even if it were conceivable— as in practice it is not—that the world (human action and the physical environment) could become a single design system, unintended consequences would persist.

The reason for this is the circularity of social knowl-edge, which affects in the first instance the social rather than the natural world. In conditions of modernity, the social world can never form a stable environment in terms of the input of new knowledge about its character and functioning. New knowledge (concepts, theories, findings) does not simply render the social world more transparent, but alters its nature, spinning it off in novel directions. The impact of this phenomenon is fundamen-tal to the juggernaut-like quality of modernity and affects socialised nature as well as social institutions themselves. For although knowledge about the natural world does not affect the world in a direct way, the circularity of so-cial knowledge incorporates elements of nature via the technological components of abstract systems.

For all these reasons, we cannot seize "history" and bend it readily to our collective purposes. Even though we ourselves produce and reproduce it in our actions, we cannot control social life completely. Moreover, the fac-tors just mentioned presume homogeneity of interest and purpose, something which one certainly cannot take for granted as regards humanity overall. The two other influences referred to previously, differential power and the roles of values, are also important. The world is "one" in some senses, but radically riven by inequalities of power in others. And one of the most characteristic features of modernity is the discovery that the development of empirical knowledge does not in and of itself allow us to decide between different value positions.

Utopian Realism

Yet none of this means that we should, or that we can, give up in our attempts to steer the juggernaut. The minimising of high-consequence risks transcends all values and all exclusionary divisions of power. "History" is not on our side, has no teleology, and supplies us with no guarantees. But the heavily counterfactual nature of future-oriented thought, an essential element of the reflexivity of modernity, has positive as well as negative implications. For we can envisage alternative futures whose very propagation might help them be realised. What is needed is the creation of models of *utopian realism*.

Simply a contradiction in terms, one might think, but such is not the case, as we can see by comparing this position to that of Marx. In Marx's version of critical theory—a theory which connects interpretation and practice—history has an overall direction and converges upon a revolutionary agent, the proletariat, which is a "universal class." Containing within itself the accumulated residue of historical oppression, the proletariat, in making the revolution, acts in the name of the whole of humanity. But history, as noted, has no teleology, and there are no privileged agents in the process of transformation geared to the realisation of values. Marx retained more than an echo of the master-slave dialectic, an outlook which is attractive because it suggests that the underprivileged are the true bearers of the interests of humanity as a whole. But we should resist such a notion, in spite of its appeal for those who struggle for the emancipation of the oppressed. The interests of the oppressed are not cut of whole cloth and frequently clash, while beneficial social changes often demand the use of differential power held only by the privileged. Moreover, many beneficial changes happen in an unintended way.

We must keep to the Marxian principle that avenues for desired social change will have little practical impact if they are not connected to institutionally immanent possibilities. It was by means of this principle that Marx distanced himself so sharply from utopianism; but those immanent possibilities are themselves influenced by the counterfactual character of modernity, and therefore a rigid division between "realistic" and utopian thought is uncalled for. We must balance utopian ideals with realism in much more stringent fashion than was needed in Marx's day. This is easily demonstrated by reference to high-consequence risks. Utopian thinking is useless, and possibly extremely dangerous, if applied, say, to the politics of deterrence. Moral conviction pursued without reference to the strategic implications of action may provide the psychological comfort which comes from the sense of worth that radical engagement can confer. But it can lead to perverse outcomes if not tempered by the realisation that, with high-consequence risks, the minimising of danger must be the overriding goal.

What should a critical theory without guarantees look

like in the late twentieth century? It must be *sociologically sensitive*—alert to the immanent institutional transformations which modernity constantly opens out to the future; it must be politically, indeed, *geopolitically, tactical*, in the sense of recognising that moral commitments and "good faith" can themselves be potentially dangerous in a world of high-consequence risks; it must create *models of the good society* which are limited neither to the sphere of the nation-state nor to only one of the institutional dimensions of modernity; and it must recognise that *emancipatory politics* needs to be linked with *life politics*, or a *politics of self-actualisation*. By emancipatory politics, I mean radical engagements concerned with the liberation from inequality or servitude. If we see once and for all that history does not obey a master-slave dialectic, or that it only does so in some contexts and circumstances, we can recognise that emancipatory politics cannot be the only side of the story. Life politics refers to radical engagements which seek to further the possibilities of a fulfilling and satisfying life for all, and in respect of which there are no "others." This is a version of the old distinction between "freedom from" and "freedom to," but "freedom to" has to be developed in the light of a framework of utopian realism.

The relation between emancipatory and life politics forms one axis of the schema shown in Figure 3. The other is that of the connections between the local and the global, so often stressed in the preceding parts of this study. Both emancipatory politics and life politics have to be tied into these connections, given the burgeoning influence of globalised relations. It is characteristic of modernity, as I have tried to show, that self-actualisation becomes fundamental to self-identity. An "ethics of the per-

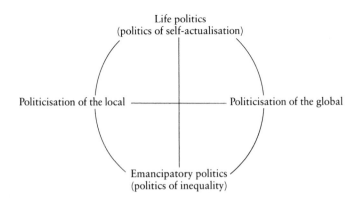

Life politics
(politics of self-actualisation)

Politicisation of the local ——————— Politicisation of the global

Emancipatory politics
(politics of inequality)

Figure 3. The dimensions of utopian realism.

sonal" is a grounding feature of life politics, just as the more established ideas of justice and equality are of emancipatory politics. The feminist movement has pioneered attempts made to connect these concerns with one another.

Theodore Roszak is justified in criticising authors, on opposing sides of the political spectrum, who see the ethos of self-discovery merely as a desperate response to the psychologically or socially inadequate character of the larger institutions of modernity. As he says, "we live in a time when the very private experience of having a personal identity to discover, a personal destiny to fulfil, has become a subversive political force of major proportions." Yet he is wrong to say that "both person and planet are threatened by the same enemy—the bigness of things."[88] What is at issue is the interlacing of distance and proximity, of the personal and the large-scale mechanisms of globalisation. "Bigness" is not in itself either an enemy of the person or a phenomenon to be overcome in life politics. Instead, it is the coordination of individual benefit and planetary organisation that has to be the focus of concern. Global connections of many kinds are the very condition of forms of individual self-actualisation, including those that act to minimise high-consequence risks.

This judgment must, in the nature of things, also apply to sectors of the world in which the impact of modernity still remains relatively weak. The transformations of the present time occur in a world riven with disparities between rich and poor states, in which the extension of modern institutions throws up all sorts of countertrends and influences, such as religious fundamentalism or forms of reactive traditionalism. If I do not consider these in detail in this book, it is for purposes of economy of argument, not because I think they can be disregarded in any more concrete interpretation of likely global trends.

Future Orientations: The Role of Social Movements

As modes of radical engagement having a pervasive importance in modern social life, social movements provide significant guidelines to potential future transformations. For those who have associated modernity above all with either capitalism or industrialism, the labour movement is the social movement par excellence. Authors who have followed Marx see the labour movement as standing in "the vanguard of history"; their critics have concentrated their attention upon showing that the labour movement only has transformative impact in the early phases of the development of an industrial order, subsequently becoming one interest group among others. To be sure, capitalism remains a class system, and the struggles of labour

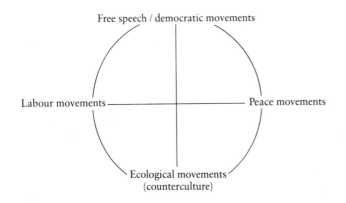

Figure 4. Types of social movements.

movements are still relevant to what might lie "beyond" it. But a single-minded preoccupation with labour movements, though at one time largely justified by their strategic importance early in the development of modern institutions and capitalistic expansion, reflects the one-sided emphasis upon either capitalism or industrialism as the sole significant dynamic forces involved in modernity. Other social movements are also important and can be connected to the multidimensional character of modernity outlined earlier.

Figure 4 should be interpreted in conjunction with Figure 1, which shows the four institutional dimensions of modernity, and essentially seen as superimposed on it. Labour movements are contestatory associations whose origins and field of action are bound up with the spread of capitalist enterprise. Whether reformist or revolutionary, they have their roots in the economic order of capitalism, specifically in attempts to achieve defensive control of the workplace through unionism and to influence or seize state power through socialist political organisation. Particularly during the relatively early phases of the development of modern institutions, labour movements tended to be major carriers of appeals for freedom of expression and democratic rights.

Yet free speech and democratic movements, which have their origins in the arena of the surveillance operations of the modern state, are analytically, and to a substantial extent historically, separable from labour movements. They include some forms of nationalist movement as well as movements concerned with rights of political participation in general. This category includes the early bourgeois associations, whom Marx regarded with some scorn as essentially class-based groups. While he was correct enough in this diagnosis, he was wrong insofar as he sought to treat "bourgeois rights" in a reductive way, solely an expression of class dominance. Such rights, and struggles to achieve, defend, or extend them, have a generic significance in modern political orders, capitalist and state socialist. Surveillance is a site of struggle in its own right.

Labour and free speech/democratic movements are "old": that is, they were well-established in certain forms prior to the current century. The other types of social movements are newer, in the sense that they have come to increasing prominence in relatively recent years. Their newness, however, can be exaggerated. Peace movements have as their site of struggle the arena of control of the means of violence, including both military and police power. "Peace" here has to be seen, like "democracy," as a contested concept central to the dialogues which such movements enter into in the fields of action they share with organisations such as the military or the state. Pacifist movements of some kinds, normally influenced by religious values, date back to the early origins of industrialised war. If they have assumed a particular significance today, this is undoubtedly in large part an outcome of the growth in high-consequence risks associated with the outbreak of war, with nuclear weaponry forming the core component in contemporary times.

The site of struggle of ecological movements—within which category countercultural movements can also be subsumed—is the created environment. Antecedent forms of today's "green" movements can also be discerned in the nineteenth century. The earliest of these tended to be strongly influenced by romanticism and basically sought to counter the impact of modern industry upon traditional modes of production and upon the landscape. Since industrialism was not immediately distinguishable from capitalism, particularly in terms of the destructive effects of both upon traditional modes of life, these groups quite often tended to be aligned with workers' movements. The separation of the two today reflects the heightened awareness of high-consequence risks which industrial development, whether organised under the auspices of capitalism or not, brings in its train. Ecological concerns, however, do not derive solely from high-consequence risks and focus also upon other aspects of the created environment.

Social movements provide glimpses of possible futures and are in some part vehicles for their realisation.[89]* But

*There is a conspicuous absence from Figure 4: feminist movements. How should we situate feminism in relation to the dimensions of modernity distinguished here and in relation to the broader discussion in the book as a whole? First, one should emphasise, feminism participates in the reflexivity of modernity just as all social movements do. Beginning from a situation in which the prime objectives were to secure rights of political and economic equality, feminist movements have come to place in question constitutive elements of gender

161

it is essential to recognise that, from the perspective of utopian realism, they are not the necessary or the only basis of changes which might lead us towards a safer and more humane world. Peace movements, for example, might be important in consciousness raising and in achieving tactical goals in respect of military threats. Other influences, however, including the force of public opinion, the policies of business corporations and national governments, and the activities of international organisations, are fundamental to the achieving of basic reforms. The outlook of utopian realism recognises the inevitability of power and does not see its use as inherently noxious. Power, in its broadest sense, is a means of getting things done. In a situation of accelerating globalisation, seeking to maximise opportunity and minimise high-consequence risks certainly demands the coordinated use of power. This is true of emancipatory politics as well as life politics. Sympathy for the plight of the underdog is integral to all forms of emancipatory politics, but realising the goals involved often depends upon the intervention of the agencies of the privileged.

The utopian streak here is obviously quite marked, and it would be shortsighted indeed to be sanguine about how

---

relations. Reflection about what gender is and how it structures basic features of personal identity are today geared to projects for profound potential transformation. Second, these concerns are closely bound up with the theme of the self as a reflexive project, for all individuals are gendered as part of the learning processes whereby a sense of self develops and is thereafter sustained or modified. Third—by virtue of this second point—some of the more deep-lying phenomena with which feminism is preoccupied are not just called into being by modernity; they are found, in one form or another, in all known forms of social order. The objectives of feminist movements are thus complex and crosscut the institutional dimensions of modernity. Yet feminism may provide sources of counterfactual thinking which contribute in a very basic way to postmodernity in the sense I am about to discuss.

far agencies of concentrated power would participate in furthering trends which might undermine their position. The interests of business corporations often diverge from those of governments, which in turn are frequently focused on sectional issues. All agendas in which there are no "others" can be redefined in terms of the pursuit of divisive concerns. Social movements are no more immune from this tendency than established organisations. Yet power is not always used for sectional gains or as a medium of oppression, and the element of realism retains its centrality.

Post-Modernity

We are currently living in a period of high modernity. What lies beyond? Can we attach any definite meaning to the concept of post-modernity? What sort of utopias can we establish, as future-oriented projects, which are connected to immanent trends of development, and therefore realistic?

I think that we can identify the contours of a post-modern order and that there exist major institutional trends which suggest that such an order could be realised. A post-modern system will be institutionally complex, and we can characterise it as representing a movement "beyond" modernity along each of the four dimensions distinguished earlier, as shown in Figure 5 (note the direct relation to Figures 1 and 4). If transformations of the kind indicated do occur, they will not automatically do so in close conjunction with one another, and a plurality of agencies would be involved were they to be realised.

What, first of all, lies beyond capitalism? If whatever it is is socialism, it is scarcely likely to bear much resem-

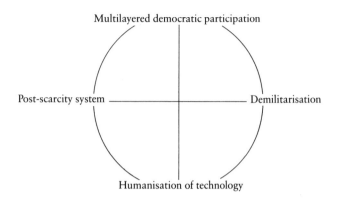

Figure 5. The contours of a post-modern order.

blance to the existing socialist societies which, while they certainly differ from capitalist states, form an economically ineffective and politically authoritarian way of managing industrialism. "Socialism," of course, means so many different things that the term is often little more than a cover-all for whatever putative social order a particular thinker wishes to see created. If socialism means rigorously planned production, organised primarily within the economic systems of nation-states, socialism is surely fading away. It is a major discovery of twentieth century social and economic organisation that highly complex systems, like modern economic orders, cannot effectively be subordinated to cybernetic control. The detailed and constant signaling such systems presuppose has to be carried out "on the ground" by low-input units, rather than guided from above.

If this holds on the level of national economies, it applies even more strongly on a worldwide level, and (as Figure 6 below indicates) we have to conceive of a post-modern era in global terms. Markets provide the signaling devices implied in complex systems of exchange, but they also sustain, or actively cause, major forms of deprivation (as Marx accurately diagnosed). Considered solely in terms of the politics of emancipation, going beyond capitalism would imply the transcendence of the class divisions which capitalistic markets bring into being. Life politics, however, points us still further, beyond circumstances in which economic criteria define the life circumstances of human beings. We find here the potential for a *post-scarcity system*, coordinated on a global level.

Simply to claim that capitalist markets must be "regulated" in order to remove their erratic qualities leads us to a dilemma. Subjecting markets to the centralised control of an all-encompassing agency is not economically efficient and leads to political authoritarianism. Leaving markets free to operate more or less without any restriction, on the other hand, produces major disparities between the life chances of different groups and regions. A post-scarcity system, however, takes us beyond this dilemma. For when the major goods of life are no longer scarce, market criteria can function solely as signaling devices, rather than being also the means of sustaining widespread deprivation.

But, we may ask, in a world characterised by massive inequalities between states and regions—especially between the industrialised and less industrialised countries—and where resources are not only finite but already under pressure, can post-scarcity be a meaningful notion? Let us ask instead, *what other alternative is there* for a world which does not pursue a self-destructive path? The pursuit of capitalist accumulation could not be carried out indefinitely, since it is not self-sustaining in terms of

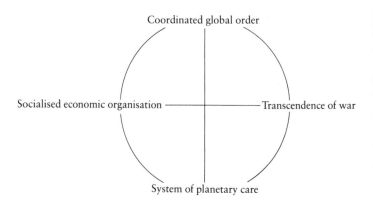

Coordinated global order

Socialised economic organisation ——————————— Transcendence of war

System of planetary care

Figure 6. Dimensions of a post-scarcity system.

resources. While some resources are intrinsically scarce, most are not, in the sense that, except for the basic requirements of bodily existence, "scarcity" is relative to socially defined needs and to the demands of specific lifestyles. A post-scarcity order would involve significant alterations in modes of social life (see Figure 6), and expectations of continuous economic growth would have to be modified. A global redistribution of wealth would be called for. Yet the motivation to produce such changes could be forthcoming, and there are many available discussions which suggest concrete policies that could be implemented to change gear in this way. There is some evidence that many people in the economically advanced states experience "development fatigue," and much evidence of a general awareness that continued economic growth is not worthwhile unless it actively improves the quality of life of the majority.[90]

A post-scarcity system, even if only developing initially in the more affluent areas of the world, would have to be globally coordinated. Socialised economic organisation on a world scale already exists in some forms—in respect of agreements between transnational corporations or national governments which seek to control aspects of the international flow of money and goods. It seems virtually certain that these will increase in years to come, whatever concrete shape they might take. If they were consolidated in the context of a transition to post-scarcity economic mechanisms, their role would presumably be more informational than regulatory. That is, they would help to coordinate global economic interchanges without playing the role of "cybernetic governor." If this sounds, and is, fairly vague, there are already available models of possible economic orders that suggest the principles which could be involved.[91]

To look at a second institutional dimension of modernity, surveillance and administrative power, certain immanent trends are also fairly clear. Within nation-states the intensifying of surveillance activities leads to increasing pressures for democratic participation (although not without pronounced countertrends). It is hardly accidental that there are virtually no states in the world today which do not call themselves "democratic," although clearly the range of specific governmental systems covered by this term is wide. Nor is this just rhetoric. States which label themselves as democratic always have some procedures for involving the citizenry in procedures of government, however minimal such involvement may be in practice. Why? Because the rulers of modern states discover that effective government demands the active acquiescence of subject populations in ways that were neither possible nor necessary in pre-modern states.[92] Trends towards *polyarchy*, defined as "the continuing responsiveness of the government to the preferences of its citizens considered as political equals,"[93] however, tend at the moment to be concentrated at the level of the nation-state. Given that the position of nation-states in the global order is changing, with new forms of local organisation proliferating at a level below it and others of an international type above it, it is reasonable to expect that new forms of democratic involvement will tend increasingly to emerge. These may take the form, for example, of pressures towards democratic participation in the workplace, in local associations, in media organisations, and in transnational groupings of various types.[94]

So far as the relations between states are concerned it seems evident that a more coordinated global political order is likely to emerge. Trends towards increasing globalisation more or less force states to collaborate over issues which previously they might have sought to deal with separately. Many of the first generation of authors to discuss globalisation, towards the end of the nineteenth century, believed that a movement to world government would naturally follow on from the development of global interconnections. Such authors underestimated the degree of sovereign autonomy of nation-states, and it does not seem likely that any form of world government resembling a nation-state "writ large" will emerge in the foreseeable future. Or, rather, "world government" might involve the cooperative formation of global policies by states, and cooperative strategies to resolve conflicts instead of the formation of a super-state. Nevertheless, the trends on this level seem strong and clear.

When we turn to the question of military power, it might appear that there is little chance of a transition to a world in which the instruments of war decline in significance. For global military expenditures continue to climb each year, and the application of innovative technology to weapons production goes on unabated. Yet there is a strong element of realism in the anticipation of a world without war. Such a world is immanent in the very process of the industrialisation of war, as well as in the altered position of nation-states in the global arena. As was mentioned earlier, Clausewitz's dictum becomes substantially obsolete with the spread of industrialised weaponry; and where the borders between nations have mostly been fixed and nation-states cover virtually the whole of earth's surface, territorial aggrandisement loses the meaning it once had. Finally, growing interdependence on a global level increases the range of situations in which similar interests are shared by all states. To envisage a world without war is clearly utopian, but is by no means wholly lacking in realism.

A similar observation applies in the case of the created environment. The constant revolutionising of technology gains some of its impetus from the imperatives of capitalist accumulation and from military considerations, but once under way has a dynamism of its own. The drive to expand scientific knowledge and to demonstrate the effectiveness of such advances in technological change is one influential factor. As Jacques Ellul points out, technological innovation, once routinely established, has a strong inertial quality:

Technology never advances towards anything *because* it is pushed from behind. The technician does not know why he is working, and generally he does not much care. . . . There is no call towards a goal; there is constraint by an engine placed in the back and not tolerating any halt for the machine. . . . The interdepdence of technological elements makes possible a very large number of "solutions" for which there are no problems.[95]

Processes of technological innovation, and of industrial development more generally, for the moment are still accelerating rather than slowing down. In the shape of biotechnology, technical advances affect our very physical makeup as human beings, as well as the natural environment in which we live. Will these powerful sources of innovation continue on unchecked for the indefinite future? No one can say with confidence, but there are some clear countertrends, partly expressed through ecological movements, but also in other spheres. Concern over environmental damage is now widespread, and a focus of attention by governments worldwide. Not just the external impact, but also the logic of unfettered scientific and technological development will have to be confronted if serious and irreversible harm is to be avoided. The humanising of technology is likely to involve the increasing introduction of moral issues into the now largely "instrumental" relation between human beings and the created environment.

Since the most consequential ecological issues are so obviously global, forms of intervention to minimise environmental risks will necessarily have a planetary basis. An overall system of planetary care might be created, which would have as its aim the preservation of the ecological well-being of the world as a whole. A possible way of conceiving of the objectives of planetary care is offered by the so-called "Gaia hypothesis" put forward by James Lovelock. According to this idea, the planet "exhibits the behaviour of a single organism, even a living creature."

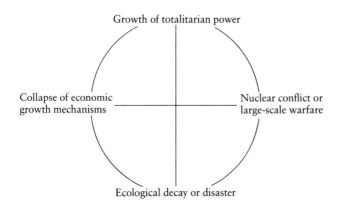

Growth of totalitarian power

Collapse of economic
growth mechanisms

Nuclear conflict or
large-scale warfare

Ecological decay or disaster

Figure 7. High-consequence risks of modernity.

The organic health of the earth is maintained by decentralised ecological cycles which interact to form a self-
sustaining biochemical system.[96] If this view can be authenticated in analytical detail, it has definite implications for planetary care, which might be more like pro-
tecting the health of a person rather than tilling a garden
in which plants grow in a disaggregated way.

Why should we assume that world events will move in
the direction outlined by these various utopian considerations? Clearly we can make no such assumption—although *all* discussions which propose such possible futures, including this one, can by their very nature make
some impact. Immanent trends of development are no
more than that, and the interim period, should things
even proceed in these various ways at all, is large and filled
with high-consequence risks. Moreover, what happens
along one institutional dimension can adversely affect
others. Each could have life-threatening consequences for
many millions of human beings.

Figure 7 sketches in the array of high-consequence

risks which we face today. Whatever new technological developments occur (which, even if beneficial for capitalistic productivity, might be dangerous for environmental safety or military security), there must be finite limits to global capitalist accumulation. Since markets are, within certain bounds, self-adjusting mechanisms, some kinds of increasing scarcity can be coped with, at least for a considerable time period. But there are intrinsic limits to the resources available for indefinite accumulation, and the "externalities" which markets either do not touch or adversely influence—such as yawning global inequalities—might prove to have socially explosive implications.

In respect of administrative resources, tendencies towards increasing democratic involvement have as their dark side possibilities for the creation of totalitarian power.[97] The intensifying of surveillance operations provides many avenues of democratic involvement, but also makes possible the sectional control of political power, bolstered by monopolistic access to the means of violence, as an instrument of terror. Totalitarianism and modernity are not just contingently, but inherently, connected, as Zygmunt Bauman in particular has made clear.[98] There are various other forms of oppressive rule which, if falling short of full totalitarian power, display some of its characteristics.

The other types of danger have been sufficiently covered in the preceding pages. The possibility of nuclear conflict is not the only high-consequence risk humanity faces in the medium-term future in respect of industrialised warfare. A large-scale military confrontation using purely conventional weaponry would be devastating in its consequences, and the continued fusion of science and weapons technology might produce other forms of armament as deadly as nuclear arms. The chance of ecological catastrophe is less immediate than the risk of major warfare, but as disturbing in its implications. Long-term, irreversible environmental damage of a serious kind might already have occurred, perhaps involving phenomena of which we are as yet unaware.

On the other side of modernity, as virtually no one on earth can any longer fail to be conscious, there could be nothing but a "republic of insects and grass," or a cluster of damaged and traumatised human social communities. No providential forces will inevitably intervene to save us, and no historical teleology guarantees that this second version of post-modernity will not oust the first. Apocalypse has become trite, so familiar is it as a counterfactual of day-to-day life; yet like all parameters of risk, it can become real.

VI

Is Modernity a Western Project?

Throughout this study, I have spoken of "modernity" without much reference to the larger sectors of the world outside the orbit of the so-called developed countries. When we speak of modernity, however, we refer to institutional transformations that have their origins in the West. How far is modernity distinctively Western? In answering this question, we have to consider various analytically separable features of modernity. In terms of institutional clustering, two distinct organisational complexes are of particular significance in the development of modernity: the *nation-state* and *systematic capitalist production*. Both have their roots in specific characteristics of European history and have few parallels in prior periods or in other cultural settings. If, in close conjunction with one another, they have since swept across the world, this is above all because of the power they have generated. No other, more traditional social forms have been able to contest this power in respect of maintaining complete autonomy outside the trends of global development. Is modernity distinctively a Western project in terms of the ways of life fostered by these two great transformative agencies? To this query, the blunt answer must be "yes."

One of the fundamental consequences of modernity, this study has emphasised, is globalisation. This is more than a diffusion of Western institutions across the world, in which other cultures are crushed. Globalisation—which is a process of uneven development that fragments as it coordinates—introduces new forms of world interdependence, in which, once again, there are no "others." These create novel forms of risk and danger at the same time as they promote far-reaching possibilities of global security. Is modernity peculiarly Western from the standpoint of its globalising tendencies? No. It cannot be, since we are speaking here of emergent forms of world interdependence and planetary consciousness. The ways in which these issues are approached and coped with, however, will inevitably involve conceptions and strategies derived from non-Western settings. For neither the radicalising of modernity nor the globalising of social life are processes which are in any sense complete. Many kinds of cultural response to such institutions are possible, given world cultural diversity as a whole. Movements "beyond" modernity occur in a global system characterised by great inequalities of wealth and power and cannot but be affected by them.

Modernity is universalising not only in terms of its global impact, but in terms of the reflexive knowledge fundamental to its dynamic character. Is modernity distinctively Western in *this* respect? This question has to be answered affirmatively, although with certain definite qualifications. The radical turn from tradition intrinsic to modernity's reflexivity makes a break, not only with preceding eras, but with other cultures. Since reason proves unable to provide an ultimate justification of itself, there is no point pretending that this break does not rest on cultural commitment (and power). Yet power does not inevitably *settle* issues that arise as a result of the spread of the reflexivity of modernity, especially in so far as modes of discursive argumentation become widely accepted and respected. Discursive argumentation, including that which is constitutive of natural science, involves criteria that override cultural differentiations. There is nothing "Western" about this if the commitment to such argumentation, as a means of resolving disputes, is forthcoming. Who can say, however, what limits might be placed upon the spread of such commitment? For the radicalising of doubt is itself always subject to doubt and therefore a principle that provokes stern resistance.

Concluding Observations

Let me attempt, in conclusion, a summary of the themes of this study. In the industrialised societies above all, but to some extent in the world as a whole, we have entered a period of high modernity, cut loose from its moorings in the reassurance of tradition and in what was for a long while an anchored "vantage-point" (both for those on the "inside" and for others)—the dominance of the West. Although its originators looked for certainties to replace preestablished dogmas, modernity effectively involves the institutionalisation of doubt. All knowledge claims, in conditions of modernity, are inherently circular, although "circularity" has a different connotation in the natural as compared to the social sciences. In the former, it concerns the fact that science is pure method, such that all substantive forms of "accepted knowledge" are in principle open to being discarded. The social sciences presume a circularity in a twofold sense, which is constitutively fundamental to modern institutions. The knowledge claims they produce are all in principle revisable, but also become "revised" in a practical sense as they circulate in and out of the environment they describe.

Modernity is inherently globalising, and the unsettling consequences of this phenomenon combine with the circularity of its reflexive character to form a universe of events in which risk and hazard take on a novel character. The globalising tendencies of modernity are simultaneously extensional and intensional—they connect individuals to large-scale systems as part of complex dialectics of change at both local and global poles. Many of the phenomena often labeled as post-modern actually concern the experience of living in a world in which presence and absence mingle in historically novel ways. Progress becomes emptied of content as the circularity of modernity takes hold, and on a lateral level the amount of daily inward information flow involved in living in "one world" can sometimes be overwhelming. Yet this is *not* primarily an expression of cultural fragmentation or of the dissolution of the subject into a "world of signs" with no centre. It is a process of the simultaneous transformation of subjectivity and global social organisation, against a troubling backdrop of high-consequence risks.

Modernity is inherently future-oriented, such that the "future" has the status of counterfactual modeling. Although there are other reasons for doing so, this is one factor upon which I base the notion of utopian realism. Anticipations of the future become part of the present, thereby rebounding upon how the future actually develops; utopian realism combines the "opening of windows" upon the future with the analysis of ongoing institutional trends whereby political futures are immanent in the present. We are returned here to the theme of time with which this work opened. What might a post-modern world be like in respect of the three sets of factors first referred to as underlying the dynamic nature of modernity? For if modern institutions are one day largely transcended, these would also necessarily become fundamentally altered. A few comments at this point will have to suffice as my conclusion.

The utopias of utopian realism are antithetical to both the reflexivity and the temporality of modernity. Utopian prescriptions or anticipations set a baseline for future states of affairs which blocks off modernity's endlessly open character. In a post-modern world, time and space would no longer be ordered in their interrelation by historicity. Whether this would imply a resurgence of religion in some form or another is difficult to say, but there would presumably be a renewed fixity to certain aspects of life that would recall some features of tradition. Such fixity would in turn provide a grounding for the sense of ontological security, reinforced by an awareness of a social universe subject to human control. This would not be a world that "collapses outward" into decentralised organisations but would no doubt interlace the local and global in complex fashion. Would such a world involve a radical reorganisation of time and space? It seems likely. With these sorts of reflections, however, we start to dissolve the connection between utopian speculation and realism. And that is further than a study of this type ought to go.

Notes

Notes

1. Jean-François Lyotard, *The Post-Modern Condition* (Minneapolis: University of Minnesota Press, 1985).
2. Jürgen Habermas, *The Philosophical Discourse of Modernity* (Cambridge, Eng.: Polity, 1987).
3. Anthony Giddens, *The Nation-State and Violence* (Cambridge, Eng.: Polity, 1985).
4. Anthony Giddens, *The Constitution of Society* (Cambridge, Eng.: Polity, 1984), ch. 5.
5. Anthony Giddens, *A Contemporary Critique of Historical Materialism* (London: Macmillan, 1981).
6. Giddens, *Nation-State and Violence.*
7. William McNeill, *The Pursuit of Power* (Oxford: Blackwell, 1983).
8. See the statistics provided in Ruth Leger Sivard, *World Military and Social Expenditures* (Washington, D.C.: World Priorities, 1983).
9. Talcott Parsons, *The Social System* (Glencoe, Ill.: Free Press, 1951).
10. I have elaborated the reasons for this in *Constitution of Society.*
11. Anthony Giddens, *New Rules of Sociological Method* (London: Hutchinson, 1974); *Constitution of Society.*
12. Eviatar Zerubavel, *Hidden Rhythms: Schedules and Calendars in Social Life* (Chicago: University of Chicago Press, 1981).
13. Stephen Kern, *The Culture of Time and Space 1880–1918* (London: Weidenfeld, 1983).
14. Giddens, *The Constitution of Society.*
15. For the critique of functionalism, see Anthony Giddens,

"Functionalism: après la lutte," in his *Studies in Social and Political Theory* (London: Hutchinson, 1977).

16. Karl Marx, *Grundrisse* (Harmondsworth: Penguin, 1973), pp. 141, 145, 166–67.

17. Georg Simmel, *The Philosophy of Money* (London: Routledge, 1978).

18. Leon Walras, *Elements of Pure Economics* (London: Allen and Unwin, 1965).

19. J. M. Keynes, *A Treatise on Money* (London: Macmillan, 1930).

20. See Alvaro Cencini, *Money, Income and Time* (London: Pinter, 1988).

21. Simmel, *Philosophy of Money*, pp. 332–33.

22. Cencini, *Money, Income and Time*.

23. R. S. Sayers, "Monetary Thought and Monetary Policy in England," *Economic Journal*, Dec. 1960; quoted in Cencini, *Money, Income and Time*, p. 71.

24. Simmel, *Philosophy of Money*, p. 179.

25. Eliot Freidson, *Professional Powers: A Study in the Institutionalization of Formal Knowledge* (Chicago: University of Chicago Press, 1986).

26. In the following discussion I have drawn upon various unpublished materials on trust made available to me by Deirdre Boden. Her ideas are of essential importance to the views I elaborate in this section and, indeed, to the book as a whole.

27. Niklas Luhmann, *Trust and Power* (Chichester: Wiley, 1979); Luhmann, "Familiarity, Confidence, Trust: Problems and Alternatives," in Diego Gambetta, ed., *Trust: Making and Breaking Cooperative Relations* (Oxford: Blackwell, 1988).

28. Luhmann, "Familiarity," p. 97.

29. *Ibid.*, p. 100.

30. Diego Gambetta: "Can We Trust Trust?" in Gambetta, *Trust*. See also the important article by John Dunn, "Trust and Political Agency," in the same volume.

31. Giddens, *New Rules*.

32. Karl Popper, *Conjectures and Refutations* (London: Routledge, 1962), p. 34.

33. Giddens, *Constitution of Society*, ch. 7.

34. Daniel Bell, *The Coming of Post-Industrial Society* (London: Heinemann, 1974).

35. Cf. Gianni Vattimo, *The End of Modernity* (Cambridge, Eng.: Polity, 1988).

36. There are many discussions in the literature of how far post-modernity should be seen simply as an extension of modernity. For an early version see Frank Kermode, "Modernisms," in his *Continuities* (London: Routledge, 1968). For later discussions see the contributions to Hal Foster, ed., *Postmodern Culture* (London: Pluto, 1983).

37. See Claude Lévi-Strauss, *The Savage Mind* (Chicago: University of Chicago Press, 1966).

38. Cf. Hans Blumenberg, *Wirklichkeiten in denen wir leben* (Stuttgart: Reclam, 1981).

39. Michel Foucault, *Discipline and Punish* (London: Allen Lane, 1977).

40. Karl von Clausewitz, *On War* (London: Kegan Paul, 1908).

41. Giddens, *Contemporary Critique*, ch. 7.

42. Daniel Bell, "The World and the United States in 2013," *Daedalus* 116 (1987).

43. See for example James N. Rosenthau, *The Study of Global Interdependence* (London: Pinter, 1980).

44. Immanuel Wallerstein, *The Modern World System* (New York: Academic, 1974).

45. Immanuel Wallerstein, "The Rise and Future Demise of the World Capitalist System: Concepts for Comparative Analysis," in his *The Capitalist World Economy* (Cambridge, Eng.: Cambridge University Press, 1979), p. 19.

46. This figure (and the discussion which accompanies it) supersedes that which appears on p. 277 of *Nation-State and Violence*.

47. H. J. Morgenthau, *Politics Among Nations* (New York: Knopf, 1960).

48. Clausewitz was a subtle thinker, however, and there are interpretations of his ideas which continue to insist upon their relevance to the present day.

49. Max Nordau, *Degeneration* (New York: Fertig, 1968), p. 39; orig. ed., 1892.

50. Georg Simmel, "The Stranger," in his *Sociology* (Glencoe, Ill.: Free Press, 1969). See also Alfred Schutz, "The Stranger: An Essay in Social Psychology," *American Journal of Sociology* 49 (1944).

51. Erving Goffman, *Behavior in Public Places* (New York: Free Press, 1963). Approaching this more directly from the point of view of trust, Alan Silver speaks of "routine benevolence" towards strangers; see his " 'Trust' in Social and Political Theory," in Gerald D. Suttles and Mayer N. Zald, eds., *The Challenge of Social Control* (Norwood, N.J.: Ablex, 1985).

52. Deirdre Boden, "Papers on Trust," mimeo. I have also profited

from Deirdre Boden and Harvey Molotch, "The Compulsion of Proximity," mimeo (Dept. of Sociology, University of California, Santa Barbara).

53. Anthony Giddens, *Central Problems in Social Theory* (London: Macmillan, 1979).

54. R. D. Laing, *The Divided Self* (London: Tavistock, 1960).

55. All quotations from Erik H. Erikson, *Childhood and Society* (Harmondsworth: Penguin, 1965), pp. 239–41.

56. D. W. Winnicott, *Playing and Reality* (Harmondsworth: Penguin, 1974), pp. 116–21. I owe a great debt to Teresa Brennan for directing my attention to his work of object-relations theory, and more generally for her advice on various sections of this book.

57. Erving Goffman, *Where the Action Is* (London: Allen Lane, 1969).

58. Giddens, *Central Problems*.

59. Harold Garfinkel, "A Conception of and Experiments with 'Trust' as a Condition of Stable Concerted Actions," in O. J. Harvey, ed., *Motivation and Social Interaction* (New York: Ronald Press, 1963).

60. Sigmund Freud, *The Future of an Illusion* (London: Hogarth, 1962).

61. Erikson, *Childhood*, p. 242.

62. Donald L. Patrick and Graham Scambler, eds., *Sociology as Applied to Medicine* (New York: Macmillan, 1982).

63. See Joshua Meyrowitz, *No Sense of Place* (Oxford: Oxford University Press, 1985); Robert D. Sack, "The Consumer's World: Place as Context," *Annals of the Association of American Geographers* 78 (1988).

64. Peter Berger, *The Homeless Mind* (New York: Random House, 1973).

65. Jürgen Habermas, *The Theory of Communicative Action*, vol. 2 (Cambridge, Eng.: Polity, 1987).

66. Max Horkheimer, *Critique of Instrumental Reason* (New York: Seabury, 1974), p. 94.

67. Claude Fischer, *To Dwell Among Friends* (Berkeley: University of California Press, 1982).

68. Sack, *Consumer's World*, p. 642.

69. See on this issue, Silver, " 'Trust' "; Alan Silver, "Friendship in Social Theory: Personal Relations in Classic Liberalism," mimeo (Dept. of Sociology, Columbia University); and Graham Allan, *A Sociology of Friendship and Kinship* (London: Allen and Unwin, 1979).

70. Ulrich Beck, "The Anthropological Shock: Chernobyl and the

Contours of the Risk Society," *Berkeley Journal of Sociology* 32 (1987).

71. Lawrence Stone, *The Family, Sex and Marriage in England 1500–1800* (London: Weidenfeld, 1977), p. 282.

72. Christopher Lasch, *Haven in a Heartless World* (New York: Basic, 1977), p. 140. See also his *The Minimal Self* (London: Picador, 1985), in which the formulation of narcissism is sharpened, and the theme of "survivalism" developed further.

73. Ulrich Beck, *Risikogesellschaft: Auf dem Weg in eine andere Moderne* (Frankfurt: Suhrkamp, 1986), p. 7.

74. Owen Green et al., *Nuclear Winter* (Cambridge, Eng.: Polity, 1985).

75. See Beck, *Risikogesellschaft*.

76. Joe Bailey, *Pessimism* (London: Routledge, 1988).

77. A. J. Jouhar, ed., *Risk in Society* (London: Libbey, 1984); Jack Dowie and Paul Lefrere, *Risk and Chance* (Milton Keynes: Open University Press, 1980).

78. Cf. W. Warren Wagar, *Terminal Visions* (Bloomington: University of Indiana Press, 1982).

79. Carolyn See, *Golden Days* (London: Arrow, 1989), p. 126.

80. Robert Jay Lifton and Richard Falk, *Indefensible Weapons* (New York: Basic Books, 1982).

81. Susan Sontag: *AIDS and Its Metaphors* (Harmondsworth: Penguin, 1989).

82. Raymond Williams, *Towards 2000* (London: Chatto, 1983).

83. Dorothy Rowe, *Living with the Bomb* (London: Routledge, 1985).

84. See, for example, J. L. Simon and H. Kahn, *The Resourceful Earth* (Oxford: Blackwell, 1984).

85. See Bailey, *Pessimism*.

86. Clifford Geertz, *Local Knowledge* (New York: Basic Books, 1983).

87. Saul Bellow, *Herzog* (Harmondsworth: Penguin, 1964), p. 323.

88. Theodore Roszak, *Person/Planet: The Creative Disintegration of Industrial Society* (London: Gollancz, 1979), pp. xxviii, 33.

89. Alberto Melucci, *Nomads of the Present* (London: Hutchinson Radius, 1989).

90. Ian Miles and John Irvine, *The Poverty of Progress* (Oxford: Pergamon, 1982).

91. William Ophuls, *Ecology and the Politics of Scarcity* (San Francisco: Freeman, 1977).

92. The rationale for this argument is given in Giddens, *Nation-State and Violence*.

93. Robert A. Dahl, *Polyarchy* (New Haven: Yale University Press, 1971), pp. 1–2.

94. See David Held, *Models of Democracy* (Cambridge, Eng.: Polity, 1987).

95. Jacques Ellul, *The Technological Society* (London: Cape, 1965), p. 89.

96. Martin Large, *Social Ecology: Exploring Post-Industrial Society* (Gloucester: Hawkins, 1981), p. 14.

97. Giddens, *Nation-State and Violence*, ch. 11.

98. Zygmunt Bauman, *Modernity and the Holocaust* (Cambridge, Eng.: Polity, 1989).